GLOBALIZATION AND THE TRANSITIONAL CULTURES

DIVERSE PERSPECTIVES ON CREATING A FAIRER SOCIETY

A fair society is one that is just, inclusive, and embracing of all without any barriers to participation based on sex, sexual orientation, religion or belief, ethnicity, age, class, ability, or any other social difference. One where there is access to healthcare and education, technology, justice, strong institutions, peace and security, social protection, decent work, and housing. But how can research truly contribute to creating global equity and diversity without showcasing diverse voices that are underrepresented in academia or paying specific attention to the Global South?

Including books addressing key challenges and issues within the social sciences which are essential to creating a fairer society for all with specific reference to the Global South, *Diverse Perspectives on Creating a Fairer Society* amplifies underrepresented voices showcasing Black, Asian, and minority ethnic voices, authorship from the Global South and academics who work to amplify diverse voices.

With the primary aim of showcasing authorship and voices from beyond the Global North, the series welcomes submissions from established and junior authors on cutting-edge and high-level research on key topics that feature in global news and public debate, specifically from and about the Global South in national and international contexts. Harnessing research across a range of diversities of people and place to generate previously unheard insights, the series offers a truly global perspective on the current societal debates of the 21st century bringing contemporary debate in the social sciences from diverse voices to light.

Previous Titles

- *Disaster, Displacement and Resilient Livelihoods: Perspectives From South Asia* by M. Rezaul Islam
- *Pandemic, Politics, and a Fairer Society in Southeast Asia: A Malaysian Perspective* by Syaza Shukri
- *Empowering Female Climate Change Activists in the Global South: The Path Toward Environmental Social Justice* by Peggy Ann Spitzer
- *Gendered Perspectives of Restorative Justice, Violence and Resilience: An International Framework* by Bev Orton
- *Social Sector Development and Inclusive Growth in India* by Ishu Chadda

- *The Socially Constructed and Reproduced Youth Delinquency in Southeast Asia: Advancing Positive Youth Involvement in Sustainable Futures* by Jason Hung
- *Youth Development in South Africa: Harnessing the Demographic Dividend* by Botshabelo Maja and Busani Ngcaweni
- *Debt Crisis and Popular Social Protest in Sri Lanka: Citizenship, Development and Democracy Within Global North-South Dynamics* by S. Janaka Biyanwila
- *Building Strong Communities: Ethical Approaches to Inclusive Development* by Ifzal Ahmad and M. Rezaul Islam
- *Family Planning and Sustainable Development in Bangladesh: Empowering Marginalized Communities in Asian Contexts* by M. Rezaul Islam
- *Critical Reflections on the Internationalisation of Higher Education in the Global South* by Emnet Tadesse Woldegiorgis and Cheryl Qiumei Yu
- *Exploring Hope: Case Studies of Innovation, Change and Development in the Global South* by Marcelo Sili, Andrés Kozel, Samira Mizbar, Aviram Sharma, and Ana Casado
- *Social Constructions of Migration in Nigeria and Zimbabwe: Discourse, Rhetoric, and Identity* by Kunle Oparinde and Rodwell Makombe
- *Rural Social Infrastructure Development in India: An Inclusive Approach* by M Mahadeva

Forthcoming Titles

- *'Natural' Disasters and Everyday Lives: Floods, Climate Justice and Marginalisation in India* by Suddhabrata Deb Roy
- *Neoliberal Subjectivity at Work: Conduct, Contradictions, Commitments and Contestations* by Muneeb Ul Lateef Banday
- *The Emerald Handbook of Family and Social Change in the Global South: A Gendered Perspective* by Aylin Akpınar and Nawal H. Ammar
- *An Introduction to Platform Economy in India: Exploring Relationality and Embeddedness* by Shriram Venkatraman, Jillet Sarah Sam, and Rajorshi Ra
- *Gender and Media Representation: Perspectives from Sub-Saharan Africa* by Margaret Jjuuko, Solveig Omland, and Carol Azungi Dralega
- *Unearthing the Institutionalised Social Exclusion of Black Youth in Contemporary South Africa: The Burden of Being Born Free* by Khosi Kubeka

GLOBALIZATION AND THE TRANSITIONAL CULTURES: AN EASTERN PERSPECTIVE

BY

DR. DEBANJANA NAG

Central Tribal University of Andhra Pradesh, India

United Kingdom – North America – Japan – India
Malaysia – China

Emerald Publishing Limited
Emerald Publishing, Floor 5, Northspring, 21-23 Wellington Street, Leeds LS1 4DL

First edition 2025

Copyright © 2025 Debanjana Nag
Published under exclusive licence by Emerald Publishing Limited

Reprints and permissions service
Contact: www.copyright.com

No part of this book may be reproduced, stored in a retrieval system, transmitted in any form or by any means electronic, mechanical, photocopying, recording or otherwise without either the prior written permission of the publisher or a licence permitting restricted copying issued in the UK by The Copyright Licensing Agency and in the USA by The Copyright Clearance Center. Any opinions expressed in the chapters are those of the authors. Whilst Emerald makes every effort to ensure the quality and accuracy of its content, Emerald makes no representation implied or otherwise, as to the chapters' suitability and application and disclaims any warranties, express or implied, to their use.

British Library Cataloguing in Publication Data
A catalogue record for this book is available from the British Library

ISBN: 978-1-83608-587-4 (Print)
ISBN: 978-1-83608-586-7 (Online)
ISBN: 978-1-83608-588-1 (Epub)

Printed and bound by CPI Group (UK) Ltd, Croydon, CR0 4YY

INVESTOR IN PEOPLE

The book is dedicated to my mentor Prof Virendra Pal Singh (Retd), *Chairman, Global Research Education Foundation India, Ex-HoD, Center for Globalization and Development Studies, University of Allahabad, Prayagraj, India, a teacher who has been a profound source of inspiration for me and taught me to fight and conquer all the obstacles that came across my path.*

CONTENTS

About the Author		*xi*
Preface		*xiii*
1.	Globalization: The Conceptual Framework	1
2.	Cultures in Transition: Through Globalization	15
3.	Communication as a Carrier of Globalization	29
4.	Transition in Communication and Cultural Change in Global South	47
5.	Cultural Globalization and the Marginal People: The Case of India	57
6.	Globalized Technologies and Modernity: An Assessment	67
7.	Epilogue: Putting the Threads Together	85
Bibliography		*89*
Index		*97*

ABOUT THE AUTHOR

Dr. Debanjana Nag is a Faculty Member at Central Tribal University of Andhra Pradesh, India. She is also the Nodal Officer for the Dr Ambedkar Center of Excellence (DACE) a scheme started by the Ministry of Social Justice, Government of India for providing free Civil Services coaching to the Scheduled Caste and marginalized students in the university. She completed her PhD in the year 2022 from the Center for Development Studies, University of Allahabad, India. Her specialization is in globalization, culture, and marginalized groups like women and tribes. She has been offered UGC – Hungaricum fellowship in the year 2022. Previously, she was engaged as a Research Associate at Govind Ballabh Pant Social Science Institute, Prayagraj. During her research period, she has also worked on various projects as a Research Assistant for different national-level bodies like National Commission for Women, the National Child Labor Project in the district Rampur of Uttar Pradesh India, etc. She also worked as a National Level Monitor for the evaluation of government schemes under the Ministry of Rural Development and Sanitation like MNREGA (rural employment program), PMAY (housing and sanitation program), etc. Till now, she has published chapters in edited books, various research papers in both English and Hindi language, and has also done some translation and transcription work for the Hindi journal "Samajikee" published by Govind Ballabh Pant Social Science Institute, Prayagraj. She has also expertise in four languages, i.e., Hindi, English, Bengali, and Assamese.

PREFACE

The book *Globalization and Transitional Cultures: An Eastern Perspective* is a thesis work that has been converted into a book. The concept of globalization is always in question. It is a concept that has prevailed for ages, but with the arrival of communication technologies and the advancement of digitalization, the impact of it has become much evitable. Most of the time, the concept has been understood in the Western views like how McDonaldization has changed the world or how technological advancements have spread Western ideologies in all parts of the globe. However, very few studies question whether globalization can popularize Eastern ideologies. The book is an attempt to resolve this question and to examine the glocalization process where the local thoughts of each ideology can be globalized and escalated in a wider platform.

To establish the ideas, the author has taken the help of both primary and secondary sources. The secondary sources include various reviews of the literature consisting of various examples, sloka or verse, the theories given by the pioneers of globalization and cultural studies to identify the gap in those studies and to understand how their views are relevant in today's world. Similarly, the help of a primary survey has been conducted to assess contemporary sociocultural values, norms, and ethics, especially in the countries of the Global South like India. All these processes took acute studies related to the field. As the book was basically a thesis, considerable revisions, modifications, and additions have been done accordingly for better representation of the book. The book has attempted to illustrate major theories and terms related to globalization and cultural aspects. Further, it also takes up the cases like tribal societies as in most of the cases being a marginalized society, their relevance is often omitted in the perspective of globalization and cultural change though they constitute a huge population in the countries of the Global South. Hence, the book is purely an attempt to understand globalization from an Eastern perspective, which is different from Western ideologies and includes marginal sections of society like tribes, women, and the middle class at large.

There is a famous saying of Albert Einstein "Education is not learning of facts, but the training of the mind to think." The book is the outcome of rigorous thinking, support, and hard work of many people. I owe to my mentor

Prof Virendra Pal Singh (Retd) earnestly for his immense help and guidance in the process of completion of this work. I thank Prof T. V. Kattimani, Vice-Chancellor, Central Tribal University of Andhra Pradesh who always encouraged me in my academic journey and stood behind me as a backbone all the time. Love to my parents Mr Sambhu Lal Nag and Mrs Anita Nag, my dearest sister Alankita Nag, and my husband Mr Vageesh Kumar Mishra for helping me to keep my morale up in my hardest times. They are the ones who lived this journey with me every single day both in good and adverse times. I also thank Emerald Publication for allowing me to present my work in front of the world in the form of this book. I hope the book will guide scholars who are working in the field of globalization, culture, and development studies.

1

GLOBALIZATION: THE CONCEPTUAL FRAMEWORK

The dawn of the 20th century evidenced the emergence of three new catchwords namely globalization, privatization, and liberalization. Among these three concepts, the concept of globalization is the most complex and challenging one. Globalization is viewed through various perspectives from epistemological, analytical, and critical to grassroots levels of civil society and public actions. Globalization was more centered on quantitative approaches like trade, tariffs, free flow of the global market system, etc. But by the beginning of the 21st century, it changed its course toward more qualitative approaches: political, demographic, environmental, or cultural.

The 20th century has been an era of many radical and theoretical changes. During the 1950s–1960's, the Marxian and Weberian debates of class and social mobility were the major topics of discussion among scholars. The decade of 1960–1970 focused on gender-based issues like feminism and inequalities. The decade of 1970–1980 was "post-modernism". Along with postmodernism, the idea of globalization got prominence in the late 80's to early 90's. With the development of interactive technologies, it soon became a buzzing phenomenon. The world gradually converted into a small village. It transformed the concept of time and space over the world. With the evolution of WEB 2.0, even the technologies that were based on one-way communication systems converted to a two-way communication system.

The major changes in the economies were witnessed, especially in developing countries like India, which became an IT hub for the developed countries for outsourcing knowledge workers. Though extractions of technical minds were ongoing, these technological developments also benefitted developing countries by producing more skilled generations. With the emerging communication system, the common people also started taking an interest in socio-political conditions and they had an opportunity to express their views. Eventually, people became more global accelerating the process of globalization. From case of economic perspective, communication technologies and cultural interactions showed immense success, whereas in terms of sociopolitical factors like lessening the decision-making rights of the national governments, developing Westernization over other civilizations, etc., were not so preferred. As a result, though globalization has become an integral part of the recent world, it remains a debatable issue.

The term "Globalization" comes from the word "globalize" referring to an increasingly borderless and interconnected world. Through the integration of capital, conservation, and acts of human rights, development, and transportation of cultural commodities, globalization is reconstructing global economic orders, consumer conscience, and cultural landscapes that have direct implications on human development.

According to Held et al. (1999, p. 2), "Globalization may be thought initially as the widening, deepening and speeding up of worldwide interconnectedness in all aspects of contemporary social life, from the cultural to the criminal, the financial to the spiritual". Held further opines that global governance is diminishing national governance and thus making nation-states irrelevant. He further argues that neither Westphalia's system of sovereign nations nor today's globe-centric system can solve the political challenges. Hence, he suggests a multilayered economy that can create an economic and sociopolitical linkage between governmental and nongovernmental organizations.

Jan Aart Scholte (2000) states that the world is going through "relative deterritorialization" and will gradually face "supra territorial relations", i.e., the process of globalization is displacing the sovereign power and control of governments over the territories, cultural practices of land, denying the international relationships between individual states and thus generating homogenous practices and relations over the supra territories.

One important concept to understand globalization is the "Minimal Phase Model of Globalization" proposed by Roland Robertson. Robertson proposed this theory in the year 1992, which describes the process of globalization through five different phases, where globalization goes through various stages from creating a change to a declining stage. In all these stages, Roland Robertson argues globalization is a very long and complicated process (Dimitrova, 2002) where changes occur at a very slow pace. Robertson is among the pioneers of globalization theory. He describes globalization as a cognitive process where an individual or a society perceives any changes through their understanding and accordingly, they accept or reject any phenomenon. This is how Robertson's theory differs from other notions of globalization based mainly on the imposed traditions of westernization and hence, he give more focus on the word glocalization rather than globalization.

Scholars like Friedman (1999) associate cultural globalization with Americanization or homogenization of culture, whereas other scholars found it as a heterogeneous process where if two cultures come into confluence both will grasp some entity from the other. As a result, the concept of multiculturalism will develop. With changing dimensions of sociopolitical interactions, the level of cultural interactions also changes. It further creates the debate of cultural homogeneity and cultural heterogeneity in the society. So, it can be visible that globalization as a cultural aspect is purely a multidimensional process.

On the other hand, John Tomlinson (1999) in his book defines globalization from the point of view of culture and describes it as the characterization of global social life that has a complex network of growing cultural interconnectedness and interdependence. He further states, "Globalization lies at the heart of modern culture, cultural practices lie at the heart of globalization." Tomlinson sees global culture as a different element from globalized cultures. He sees global culture as a result of influenced culture or a single-world culture, whereas he defines the term globalized culture as a culture that constructs identities of different cultures at a global level. Thus, he defines globalization helps in the construction of a globalized culture rather than a global culture.

Goran Therborn (1995) sees globalization as a wave of evolving civilizations and he argues that as civilizations are developed, along with evolves the process of globalization. For example, with industrialization, concepts like division of labor, world trade, world market, interdependence, world production rights, world influence, universal law/rights, capital/income, world impact, world finance, world market, determination of risks/opportunity, etc. evolved. With the evolution of "world culture" systems, identities, cross-continental interchange, world diffusion values, world influences, world religions or ideologies, universal homogenization/hybridization, etc. came into context. Thus, Therborn sees globalization as a hand-in-hand phenomenon of culture and establishes cultural globalization as one of the major discourses of globalization.

Turner and Khondker (2010) in the book "Globalization East or West" talks about the changing notion of globalization with context of East and West. It tries to understand the eastern matters that are seeing constant transformations due to coming in contact with the western world. The book analyzes the affect more in an economic and political scenario and brings about the perspectives of other scholars like Amartya Sen who believes, "Globalization is neither Western nor Eastern (Turner & Khondker, 2010, p. 45)." For this, it explains the concepts of universal knowledge systems like the science of mathematics, geography, etc. to establish its theory. However, if seen in a more acute way, it is seen that when dived down more deeply into the cultural affairs, the elements of globalization create different impacts on different cultures. This makes it more important to understand the effects of cultural globalization separately for the Eastern and Western world.

B. Axford's edited book, "Why Globalization Matters?" (2021) takes up various questions of globalization in different chapters. It talks about various disciplines of globalization including political science, sociology, geography, anthropology, and communication studies, etc. and how theoretical approaches to globalization like space, culture, history, governance, and capitalism work as an umbrella term to create complex interconnectedness among these approaches (Theiner, 2014).

Manuell Castells in his "The Rise of Network Societies" (1996) articulates a weaker section of power, i.e., "influence." He states, "the nation-state is losing power but not influence." He further discusses that due to it societies, today are reshaping and reforming new linkages. He termed it as "Network Societies," which means the power in the globalized world has been diffused in many intersecting networks rather than in a single state. Hence, it can be said that globalization in politics has restructured world institutions, and some critics argue that it has turned the political agencies toward a cosmopolitan democracy.

The new type of society is in the phase of postmodernism and is hugely *globalized* and the rise of concepts like Manuell Castells's (1991) "The Rise of Information Society", and Marshall McLuhan's "The Global Village" (1964), etc. has helped in the formation of a new type of social systems. Thus, the new social system concentrates more on global problems rather than on individuals. The availability of free and quick information is a major factor behind this that eventually progresses the process of globalization. Singh (2004) argues, "The effects of Globalization started with the 'cultural invasion from the sky' is now centered on 'the emergence of information society'. Hence, it can be said that the era of globalization centrally depends upon the flow of information."

Anthony Giddens (1996) describes that the process of globalization is going through four layers: extensification, or the process of stretching social relations; intensification, or the intensifying rate of world trade system and exchanges; velocity, or the speeding up of global flows; and the impact that can be visualized due to global interconnectedness. Since the beginning of modernization, trends of change have been flourishing in the society. Globalization as a process brought likeliness to the lifestyle of people through their food, fashion, art, and music, even in the process of thinking. It created a background for diminishing plurality and forming a homogenized and liberalized world. Further, globalization turned into a *"process of change"* that is spread over various aspects of society economic, political, demographic, cultural, technological, and environmental.

Globalization in all of its forms therefore can be said to be a transition from the traditional period of history to the modern age of discontinuity. It is the extension of society and interconnection between the societies that covers the whole globe. Interactive technologies are fueling its growth process, and its institutional dimension can interlink the cross-border flow of social and cultural artifacts. With the cross-border flow of sociocultural elements, the globe thus experiences a journey toward a more rational and modern world. To study and discuss this process of change through globalization, three different schools based on three different perspectives have been established. These schools of globalization are discussed elaborately in the following section.

SCHOOLS OF GLOBALIZATION

Based on the nature of globalization, it has been mainly divided into three major schools: Hyperglobalizers, Skeptics, and Transformationalists.

Hyperglobalizers

Hyperglobalization was a term that came into existence in the early 1990s. It was used to describe the "rapid rise of trade integration". Eventually, it became a dynamic school that believed globalization is a process that can create integration among all global-level procedures, i.e. trade, culture, communication, etc. According to the hyperglobalizers, globalization has ended the concept of nation-states and made it irrelevant. Rather it has created a *global village* amplifying the concepts of internationalism and cosmopolitanism. The hyperglobalizers can be again subdivided into positive hyperglobalizers and negative hyperglobalizers.

Kenichi Ohmae's book "Borderless World" (1990) supported positive hyperglobalizers. He stated that "a fundamental paradigm shift" is going on in the international market. He discusses this shift with the fact that as the flow of goods and services has become much easier after the emergence of GATT, it is not possible to attach the countries with a "single economic unit" only. According to him, this easier flow of goods and services is also creating a "dispersion of economies" as they can trade globally with much flexibility. To ensure that these flows of goods and services can run smoothly, he also suggests a global governing body that can regulate the "global flow of economy ending the nation-states boundaries". His argument can be further explained by Daniel Bell's "The End of Nation-States." He also supports the school arguing that diminishing geographical boundaries has also diminished the usefulness of international laws.

The "negative hyperglobalizers" on the other hand were mainly the Neo-Marxist scholars like James. C. Scott. They are the critiques of globalization. They find globalization as "expansionist capitalism" or a kind of "imperialism." James C. Scott in his article "Vernaculars Cross-Dressed as Universals: Globalization as North Atlantic Hegemony" (2009) believes "globalization may eliminate, diminish, or replace: vernacular practices such as the cultures, religions, and languages of less numerous peoples, local forms of agriculture and land tenure, and other ways of life and institutions that appear to stand in the way of standardization."

The opinions of negative hyperglobalizers have further helped in the rise of the *"Standardization thesis of Globalization"* as pioneered by James. C. Scott (1998) in his thesis. It comprehends globalization as a process by which the capitalists control the world by hegemonizing nation-states, creating monoculture, and conglomerating Multinational Companies. It standardizes the complex societal norms, tacit vernacular practices, and precious indigenous cultures. Hence, the hyperglobalizers view globalization as a totally "homocentric" notion.

Skeptics

With the emergence of Globalization, the concept of *deterritorialization* emerged and the school of hyperglobalizers pivoted in this concept. However, the concept was rejected by the skeptics school of globalization as they opined that globalization is not based on the concept of one nation, one government rather it segments the world into major regional blocs. The skeptics' school of globalization states that neither globalization is a new concept, nor it has created an epochal transformation in international affairs. Rather it has segmented the world economies into smaller regional blocs. The skeptics believe globalization is an advanced mode of *Western imperialism*. They found it a concern of powerful states and without their hegemony, the contemporary world system would decree. On account of this, the skeptics' beliefs are divided into two methodological models:

The first model opines that globalization has articulated the world into three major blocks, i.e. the European Union, North America, and Asia, especially Japan. The whole current world economy is surrounded by these three blocks. Waltz (1999) states that globalization is not global at all but is mainly divided into northern latitudes. The results can be seen in the case of the expansion of McDonalds' in far-ranging places with the popularization of Facebook, and Twitter among all sections of society; from considering hamburgers, pizzas, cokes, and sandwiches as favorite past time meal to accepting Sushi as a quality cuisine across the world; the influence of the regional blocks is crystal clear.

The second methodological concept argues that globalization is not ending the nation-states, but they are as strong as ever before. The openness in world trade before World War I was much higher, likewise global flows in economies and global migration flows were also higher in the 19th century as compared to today. Henceforth, the skeptics like Hirst and Thompson (1996) prefer the term *Internationalization* over globalization.

Transformationalists

The transformationalists, who are the third school of globalization, are considered to be the most prominent school of globalization. Transformationalists believe that globalization is not a teleological process. It is an absolute phenomenon. The effects of globalization are not only limited to economic or political activities but also reflexive in the arenas of technology, environmental aspects cultural artifacts, etc. They believe that the concept of nation-states is still effective and cannot be diminished. David Held (1999) argues that only the shape of nation-states has been restructured by global governance, international laws, and social movements. The territorial boundary still exists but now global monetary flows and other economic activities are more accessible to foreigners and investors. Thus, the sovereignty of the nation-states is under threat as they are shared.

Transformationalists believe that nation-states are an integral part of the sociopolitical system and thus the world can never be homogenized or segmented. Transformationalists also state that the flow of culture is not a one-way process. Westernization has not swallowed up the local cultures. It has also been influenced by them. Local cultures may lose some of their heterogeneity but will always have their own presence in the ongoing society resulting in the process of glocalization where there is an immense scope to expand the local thoughts and artifacts to go global. The establishment of

ISKCON temples in the hearts of North America by Bhaktivedanta Swami Prabhupada and the spread of Hare Krishna movement that still attracts the Western Community toward the pages of Shrimad Bhagwat – Gita, in the land of Mathura-Vrindavan or in the Ghats of Varanasi is the finest example of how a local tradition can be recognized throughout the globe heartily.

Hence, globalization is a two-way exchange and the only change that has taken place is the concept of culture that is now less stable as hybridized global identity has been overwhelming the recent world. Thus, all three schools have their own ideological concepts and based on this each one of them has their own notion to look upon the approaches of globalization.

APPROACHES OF GLOBALIZATION

In the theory of "Discontinuities of Modernity," Anthony Giddens argues that whenever the development of any process occurs, along with comes the different phrases through which the development process comes to its original shape. These are the transitional phrases in which society comes under stress and as a result, different kinds of discontinuities are generated. These various forms of discontinuities further create various kinds of approaches to that process and thus the process of development takes place. Based on this theory of Anthony Giddens, the processes of globalization are substantially influenced by four major sets of approaches specifically.

Globalization as a Time–Space Approach

The link between time–space and globalization can be found in David Harvey's "The Condition of post-modernity" (1989). He coined the term "Time-Space Compression" to describe that if there is an acceleration in economic activities in the world, there follows the destruction of spatial cross-borders and distances automatically. With increasing communication and technology, the capital moves to the transnational boundaries at a much wider and faster level. He believes that compression of time and space is a key factor behind globalization.

The concept of time–space in building blocks of globalization has also grabbed attention in Anthony Giddens' "Time-space distanciation." His major thinking was that social relations get stretched over space and time. The expansion of global media, information technology, and transportation has changed the historical trajectories of different societies. For instance: tribal society due to lack of modernity has been less globalized, whereas the class-divided and industrialized societies are much underpinned by it. Manuell Castells (1991) argues that information and technology have increased global informational capitalism. Due to these social relations are coming together "Sharing time" across all physically distant places at a simultaneous time and space.

Globalization as a Territory-Scale Approach

Saskia Sassen (1991) concentrates on two phenomena of globalization, i.e. territory and scale. It is based upon transborders or "deterritorialization". According to it, social relations are detaching from their place of origin to the place of destination. Again, it can happen on a multiscalar basis, i.e. from local to regional, regional to national, and national to global, etc. Dicken (2007) divided this approach of globalization into four multiscalar processes: localizing process, i.e. concentrated over various function integrated activities, internationalizing, i.e. spread over simple geographical national borders with a low level of economic activities, regionalizing, i.e., spread over supranational scale and finally globalizing, i.e., spread over extensive geographical areas and high-level economic activities. Thus, the exchange of ideas on different scalar bases can contribute to the expansion of globalization at a vascular stage.

Globalization as a System-Structure Approach

Immanuel Wallerstein's (2000, 2004) work states that globalization is occurring more systematically and structurally. History evidences many mini-economic systems, but contemporary societies are more systematic as they are under a "single whole" economic system. It includes a single market economy and a three-tier political structure. He segmented the capitalist world economy into three-tier structural processes, i.e. the core, the periphery, and the semiperiphery. He developed the concept of the "middle class" through the semi-periphery to maintain the political balance. The semiperiphery exploits the periphery simultaneously is exploited by the core. Hence, it can be said that the interconnectedness of the societies is undertaking at a meso-level and is influencing globalization more systematically and structurally.

Globalization as a Process-Agency Approach

Globalization is widely processed in nature. Micheal Hardt and Antonio Negri (2000) in "The Empire" thesis argue that globalization processes are not limited to a "single latitude' but rather sustained through multitudes. For example, if one empire expands immensely, there emerges a counter-empire to control it.

Same way, every political organization faces an alternative organization to look over its global flows and exchanges. The system is not limited only to political organizations but also consists of the movement of information, capital, people, or culture. For example, expansion of Buddhism from India and felicitation as one of the most acceptable religions of South Asia, the movement of Indian Diasporas to the foreign land has created a Pan-Indian culture in that region. Many Indian words like Bungalow, Jungle, Loot, Dacoit, etc. have replaced the original words used for them in English vocabulary. The elements that are present today came after discarding some previous forms of traditions and there will also be some traditions in the future that will again refuse the existing processes. Thus, there can be many agencies that are processing globalization. Hence, it can be viewed that time and space, territory and scale, system and structure, process and agency are the four main building blocks of globalization.

PROCESSES OF GLOBALIZATION

Singh, V.P. (2004) states, "The process of globalization can be analyzed at two levels: globalization as a structural process and globalization as a cultural process." As a structural process, globalization stratifies the social structures, economic and legal institutions, religious structures, educational and media institutions, etc. As a cultural process, globalization showcases culture as the cultivation of intricate social actions that occur globally. It concentrates on the integration, convergence, and diffusion of cultural traits. Globalization has been visualized as an infrastructure of cultural production, cultural transmission, and cultural reception. It can be further described as.

Globalization as a Structural Process: Include Economic and Political Process

The economic and political processes are the most important dimensions that transform the structure of society most rapidly. The impact of globalization on these structural variables can be defined further as follows.

Economic Process

In economic spheres, globalization is the wide acceptance of free markets and global flows with fewer tariffs or barriers. Economic globalization focuses on increasing the quality of human life by increasing the size of capital flows, foreign investments, and converting local commodities to international products. It works for the betterment of economic opportunities by increasing the flow of information. The major factor behind the rise of economic globalization was the emergence of liberalization. With a rising global market, the world followed a global migration flow. The immigration from poorer regions to developed regions fueled the expansion of worldwide capitalism.

If we go through *historical perspectives,* the first step toward economic globalization was taken by the Bretton Woods Commission in 1944. The commission created a stable currency exchange system by fixing gold values with US dollars. Gradually, to regulate the global monetary functions institutional agencies like the International Monetary Fund (IMF) in 1945 and the establishment of GATT (General Agreement on Tariffs and Trade) in 1947, etc. were formed. Later, it enforced the foundation of the World Trade Organization (WTO) in 1995 as a successor to the above. By that time, other regional trading blocs like the European Union, NAFTA, SAARC, etc. also came into existence. In 1997, there was a slight change in the model of Western Capitalism, and South Asian countries like Japan, China, India; etc. were the new global markets for the World Economic system. Along with Transnational Corporations (TNC's) also ensured that cheap availability of labor, resources, and manufacturing facilities can be provided to the other regions of the world. Global Marketing companies like Nike, H&M, Zara, etc. were dependent on Asian countries like India, Vietnam, Indonesia, South Korea, Taiwan, etc., for sources of raw materials, market, and manufacturing.

Here again comes the most debatable question from Gunnar Myrdal (1968). He raises the question of whether Economic Globalization is meant only for developed or capitalist countries or is it the cores that are using the peripheries and semi-peripheries for their economic development making the latter poorer or does the peripheries also benefit from the outcomes of Globalization? The answer can be searched in Amartya Sen's concept of 'Capability Approach' (1979), which identifies the main reasons for Poverty and Inequality. According to the approach, even a rich country can have a poor due to unequal distribution of wealth. It is not the cores that are depriving the peripheries of development rather poverty is caused by ignorance, government oppression, lack of financial resources, and other value-based systems that can only be gained by formulating social justice, equality, and increasing the quality of life.

Thus, financial institutions and their liberalization contributed to an explosive rate of growth in the world economy. Productions of goods were done at the global level and the concept of "Global commodity chain" flourished. Thus, the economic dimensions of globalization manifested global market connectedness intensifying the globe to be more interdependent.

Political Process

Aside from the economic perspectives, the major debate on globalization is political processes. Neo-Marxist scholars like Caroline Thomas (2001) argue that now power is located in global society formations and expressed through global networks rather than territorially based states and the expression of the global economy is the result of acceptance of international restrictions by local political bodies. The most conflicting issue in political globalization is the fate of the nation-states. According to the market principles, the concept of "global governance" or "a single market economy" has almost made the nation-states powerless. Free trade markets have made society more open by placing restrictions on the power of the local Government. Here the question arises whether the growing intergovernmental organizations with their restrictive principles of trade and economic policies have affected the sovereignty of the nation states. The end of nation-states somehow appears to be a weapon of capitalist economies to persist in their domination over the developing and less-developed countries indirectly through a variety of means.

MNCs and Unfair Global trade are one of the strongest forces to establish neo-colonialism. They often try to gain control over the natural resources and impose unequal agreements to bind them to withdraw subsidies from important sectors like agriculture further creating risks for the locales to lose their land and thus impede the development of the other national economies that again lead them to the status of peripheries. International Aid, Structural Adjustment Programs, and Importing Expertise are also some of the methods through which international institutions like IMF put lots of conditions to provide aid like withdrawing social security from the recipient country making it vulnerable to the donator country. Hugo Chavez, the former President of Venezuela, considered humanitarian aid as a major political weapon of the capitalist economy.

Political globalization has become a question of debate for scholars whether it makes the world more humanitarian or whether it is a trouble for the new world system. The exit of Britain from the European Union or BREXIT is one such phenomenon that ignores global governance and focuses more on the sovereignty of the nation-states. Hence, globalization can minimize the influence of nation-states, but it is not possible to withdraw the concept of nation-states totally from the world system of politics.

Globalization as a Cultural Process

The globalization of culture is the oldest and most important process of all. The root of cultural globalization is not new but can be seen even in the pages of history. Globalization as a cultural process is the study of culture from both material and nonmaterial perspectives. From the prospect of globalization, culture is the cultivation of intricate social actions that occur globally. It concentrates on the *integration, convergence,* and *diffusion* of cultural traits.

From the earlier period people from distant lands used to explore new prospects of life, especially through traveling. They passed different geographical and cultural borders for trade, but that eventually led to the process of interculturation and cross-border relationships. People from rural areas started moving toward urbanization in search of better living conditions, which led to urbanization of the society. This process was long and we too can find historical examples of the silk route, and the Indus Valley civilization where processes of trade from faraway places like Mesopotamia were creating *Cultural Integration* among different societies.

Instances of globalization of religion again led to *Cultural Convergence* that is visible in the journey of Asoka to the whole of Southeast Asia to expand Buddhist ideologies, expand of Roman Empire, and strengthen the church during those consequent periods. During the independence period of India, the expansion of Buddhist ideologies among lower castes by Dr B. R. Ambedkar as a protest movement against the caste system of Hinduism is also an example of the development of the new traits of *Cultural Convergence.* Though the primary conduits of the Globalization of culture seem to be convergence, later the impact was the cultural diffusions.

The emergence of new ideologies and thoughts as a result of the Protest movements and Bhakti movements created a new outlook among the people of different castes and classes. As a result, the people who earlier used to believe in a single ideology of Hinduism are now open to more pathways leading to the *Cultural Diffusion* or "Clash of Civilizations" as depicted by Samuel Huntington (1996). These processes of cultural integration, convergence, and diffusion were not only limited to a single community, religion, or group but their impact can be seen among all the existing communities of the world.

In the case of Islam too, the process of Westernization has created a string of acculturation, especially among Islamic countries like the United Arab Emirates, Turkey, etc. where the sky touching roofs, luxury hotels, and buildings are meant either for professional business talks or luxury or fun. It has no connection with the basic Islamic traits of *Sharia* or other religious constraints. This clearly shows an impact of both cultural integration and cultural convergence among Islamic countries too that again leads to a prospect of cultural diffusion among the traditional Islamic communities of Afghanistan, Pakistan, etc., and globalized Islamic countries as mentioned above.

In the case of Christianity too, the ideologies of the globalization process started with the expansion of colonialism. Besides, the process of cultural globalization is not only limited to the globalization of religion but can be seen in every sphere of life, i.e. in music, art, food, lifestyle, etc.

SUMMARY

Thus, globalization as a cultural process is more dominant in the Eastern perspective, which covers a large part of the global south. The perspective here can be referred to as the viewpoint through a position or a place of an object. This is the reason a perspective is always dynamic and in the globalization process, nothing is universal or absolute. It changes with time, place, and people. Hence, globalization is a concept highly contextual in nature and depends on developmental discourses and systematic structural changes. In cultural aspects, sometimes it focuses on collaboration, decommodification, and going away from profit maximization philosophy, whereas, at other times, it creates dependence on each other and creates competition in material cultures. All these cases lead us to the fact to broaden our horizons to understand the processes of globalization and its impact on cultural transitions especially in the Eastern perspectives. To understand the process of cultural globalization, it is needed to study the concept of culture in broad in the upcoming chapters.

2

CULTURES IN TRANSITION: THROUGH GLOBALIZATION

Culture refers to the characterization of a particular region, people, their lifestyles, and habits. It focuses on the customs, norms, values, and other societal behaviors. E.B Tylor defines "Culture as that complex whole which includes knowledge, belief, art, morals, law, custom, and any other capability acquired by man as a member of society" (Tylor, 1871, p. 1). Ralph Linton defines society as "an organized group of individuals and a culture is an organized group of learned responses characteristic of a particular society" (Linton, 1955, p. 29). Majumdar and Madan (2008) say that a culture complex is not an institution but is the outcome of interaction between several institutions.

Arjun Appadurai (1996) in his essay divided the global cultural flow into five major landscapes. They are "Ethnoscapes," i.e., when people shift from one place to another in the form of tourists, refugees, immigrants, or exiles. "Technoscape," i.e., flow of technology at a greater speed. It results in the transmission of cultures through modern communication technologies globally. "Financescape" or the distribution of the global monetary system. It can flow in the form of money, trade, goods, and commodities, etc. "Mediascapes" is the formation and dissemination of mass media and how it creates interaction among different cultural identities. And last, "Ideoscapes" can be seen as the global flow of political ideas. It agitates versatile notions of political ideas like human rights, freedom, social movements, human welfare, etc. at a broader level. Thus, Appadurai's perspective tries to create a bridge between cultural aspects of society and globalization through a series of scapes. Ghosh (2011) defines culture as "in the contemporary world, culture is shaped in such a way that it adheres to the dictates of the market and utilizes customs, practices, and rituals for its benefits." He further stresses the fact that the culture of today is a consumer culture, and the market impacts the transformation of cultural components immensely.

Thus, culture has many elements subdued in it that further give rise to a new civilization based on its contemporary nature. The concepts of "civilization" and "culture" are interrelated and often complement each other along sometimes become each other's substitute also. Hence when understanding the concept of culture, it becomes necessary to clarify the difference between civilization and culture.

Ogburn and Nimkoff (1947) define "civilization as the latter phase of culture. It is a highly developed organization, a complex and more evolved form of culture. When a human society develops a certain social and political organization, it is called a civilization. Cultural is internal but civilization is external as it is the external manifestation or the material aspect of culture such as the scientific and technological achievements." Tai (2003) argues that "whereas civilization is the universal development of human beings and society, culture indicated particularity, each person has their culture and society own culture. Civilization is a much broader concept as compared to culture as it is spread beyond boundaries." Sharma (2003) argues that "All societies have cultures but all societies are not civilizations."

Majumdar and Madan (2008) describe that "culture is the moral, spiritual and the intellectual attainments of man. It stands for symbols and values. But civilization is secondary or it is something outside us. It is the sum total of the instruments of cultural life." Mauss (1954) defines "civilization as a social entity in which states and cultural forms are mutually co-present and co-extensive and yet irreducible to one another." Durkheim (1915) states that "civilizing process does not occur at the level of everyday life, which is characterized by fragmentation and heterogeneity; it is constituted rather through a society's collective ethos, which is gathered, condensed and represented in symbolic forms." Lucien Febvre and the Annales School (1930) have conceptualized civilization as the intersection and long history of the multiple forms of human life within specific (although often extensive) geographical settings. Weber (1998) differentiates civilization from the social and cultural process and argues that the civilization process refers to the "internal historical development of cultural forms." He argues that the civilization process occurs through social and cultural continuity. Thus, it can be argued that for the development of a civilization, the development of social systems and culture is necessary.

EVOLUTION AND TYPES OF CULTURE (FOLK CULTURE TO URBANIZATION, I.E., RURAL–URBAN CONTINUUM)

The human society was nomadic and primitive at its early stage and it stepped toward development with the use of tools. It was the use of tools only that led them to develop agriculture and with the development of agriculture they learned to settle down in a specific place. This was the first step toward developing a society and once they became the social animal, they established various types of cultural norms and values to run their social system in an organized way. This was the building stone of village culture. Now the primitive and nomads were settling down in villages with the help of agricultural development. With commercialization, the exchange of goods and services and the establishment of a market occurred that further encouraged them toward technological development. With the growth of industrialization and urbanization, they learned to use different types of machinery and it led to the replacement of agricultural communities at large; forming more technological, economic, and political mass organizations. Now societies are moving toward urbanization and thus migration from rural to urban areas has started taking place. In other words, this system of continuous development from one specific culture to others, i.e. folk to rural and rural to urban came to be known as the "Rural–Urban Continuum."

Robert Redfield (1941) for the first time developed this concept of the "Rural–Urban continuum" and defined it as an integral part of the culture as a "popular conceptual tool to classify different types of community and the transition between them". He described it as the newer form of culture where with the rapid process of development of information technology, the rapid process of urbanization takes place. In other words, the relationship between the development of human society and types of culture can be shown in Fig. 1.

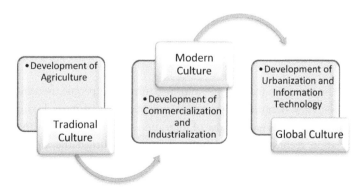

Fig. 1. Development of Human Society and Types of Cultures.

Based on it Majumdar and Madan (1956) divided the cultures primarily into three types:

Traditional Culture

According to it, the society at its primary stage is a folk/tribal society that is nomadic. Their technology was also very primitive. This type of culture was primarily based on shifting agriculture and accordingly their migration was both in linear and circulatory patterns. In linear pattern, they used to leave the agricultural field and move ahead toward a new field while in circulatory pattern they used to come back in the same field after rotation in a gap of 12 years. For example, the Mizo tribes in India were developed in a linear pattern of shifting culture that reached India by moving from regions like China and Burma, etc. One of the basic characteristics of this folk society is they are heterogeneous, and their culture is very flexible and changes rapidly with the waves of time. They don't have very rigid social systems and they belong to a diffusion culture.

Modern Culture

With changing times, the folk culture adopted technologies like plowing, sowing, harvesting, or domestication of pet animals and thus settled down in a particular place from nomads. Thus rural society came into existence and clustered development occurred. Many institutions like panchayats, village locks, etc. developed. These changes in culture also occurred. Now these societies had a systematic form of lifestyle, and their social system became rigid. They preferred to live in gatherings. Many social norms, values, and beliefs arose, and thus rural culture developed. With commercialization and industrialization, their diffusion was now toward urban cities where they got better living opportunities. Thus, the modern culture developed.

Global Culture

With the increase in technology and urbanization, people become more informative. They became highly social and in search of more luxuries and higher living standards global flow of migration occurred. New advancements in information technologies and network societies turned the world into a "global village". With this, the components of culture not only remained limited to their own region, but worldwide cultural elements also became a constituent of their culture. The cultures transformed into "global culture".

Besides the tangibility of culture, Ogburn and Nimkoff (1964) for the first time gave the concept of material and nonmaterial culture. They define it as "the elements of non-material culture are more resistant to change than the material culture. They refer to the term 'cultural lag' to refer to the maladjustment in which non-material culture fails to adjust to the rapidly changing material conditions." While material culture visualizes the culture, i.e. physically embedded like the patterns of consumption, artifacts, and other substantial properties; nonmaterial culture is the expression of ideas, values, norms, etc. While the material culture is very flexible and tangible and can be further divided into four levels, i.e. global level, national level, regional level, and local level; the nonmaterial culture is somewhat rigid and unmovable. It is mainly norm and value-based in approach. For example, the methods of worship of deities in Hinduism have been the same since the ages. It is purely based on the *Vedic Mantras* and *Puja Vidhis* (rituals) and has not witnessed any form of change along with the upcoming generations. India has gone through almost 200 years of colonization when British missionaries were a very strong organization and worked for the development of Christianity in the country, but it is the belief system of that certain community for which their success rate was very low and can't be altered so easily.

The material culture, on the other hand, has experienced immense transformations over time. At the global level, it has the world that has evidenced the globalization of fashion accessories with brands like Nike, Adidas, UCB, Levies, etc.; the globalization of food culture like Sushi, Hamburgers, Sandwiches, etc.; the globalization of tourism like OYO properties, Booking.com, the globalization of communication technologies like Facebook, Zoom, Twitter, etc. At the national level, if one looks at the Indian scenario, many brands like Haldirams, Bikaner, Peter England, Pantaloons, etc. can be found that have their own established market throughout the country. At the regional level, the material culture is restricted to some definite regions of the country like Mr. Idli in South India and Sagar Ratna in Northern India. Finally, the local level includes such brands that are doing well at a local level and have further scope to expand their market at the regional level and furthermore. The expansion of the local level to the global can also be termed as the process of glocalization. The process to localize the global culture or to globalize the local culture both creates transitions in culture. Hence, it becomes important to understand the role of globalization as a process of cultural change.

GLOBALIZATION IN TRANSFORMING THE PROCESSES OF CULTURE

The study of culture as a part of globalization is qualitative in approach and globalization directly acts as an infrastructure of cultural production, cultural transmission, and cultural reception, where one culture welcomes the element of another culture and receives it warmly as a part of their culture. For example, the use of jeans throughout the world as common attire. In all these processes, globalization of communication and information plays a vital role. Besides, According to Nederveen Pieterse (2004), cultural globalization is dominated by three views: cultural homogenization, cultural differentialism, and cultural hybridization. And all these three processes of cultural globalization are very much evident in the Global South.

Cultural Homogenization

The concept of cultural homogenization refers to creating sameness among all cultural worlds. It is a notion especially supported by hyperglobalizers who believe that due to globalization a homogeneity is being created in the entire globe. The process of cultural homogenization occurs mainly through three major notions, i.e. *cultural imperialism, mcDonaldization,* and *expansionalism.*

The concept of *cultural imperialism* came with the concept of colonialism where the dominant culture suppresses the local culture and thus establishes its own cultural regime. For example: during British India, the spread of British tea company created a ritual of having Morning tea, especially among the *Bhadraloks* of that period that later became a household ritual for all the Indian society irrespective of religion, caste, and class. It replaced the traditional nature of breakfast with some Imperial nature of Breakfast, i.e. with tea, sandwiches, toast, etc.

The notion of *McDonaldization* of society came into being with the establishment of McDonald's in most of the World's regions thus creating the reign of capitalist society over the others. It signifies the consumerist and capital-making production of culture through its technological efficiency and time-saving nature. Asian countries are one of the biggest markets for McDonaldization apart from the West and the fast-moving markets are rapidly growing in these regions as a part of material culture.

Along with this, the concept of *Expansionalism* comes hand in hand again concentrating on the fact that with the increment in McDonaldization process, the Western profit making MNC's enter into the developing and less developing cultures and thus, overpower the other cultural realm changing the previous cultural traits of the region. Hence, the concept of cultural homogenization is highly debatable as it destroys the ethnicities of local cultures and indirectly produces neo-colonialism in society. It can hamper the sovereignty of the dependent country and uphold the dominant country.

Cultural Differentialism

The concept of Cultural Differentialism was given by Huntington in 1996 in his paper "Clash of Civilizations." According to the paper, a culture can't be homogenized totally and there will be some differences always among the cultures. Sometimes it will be among other cultural religions and ideologies like Hinduism, Islam, Christianity, etc., or capitalism or socialism, and sometimes among the own cultural ideologies like Mahayana or Hinayana among Buddhism, Shvetambaras and Digambaras in Jainism, etc. that belong to same ideology but still has some differences. The cultural differentialism takes place primarily through *Traditionalism* and *Pluralism.*

The notion of traditionalism refers to strengthening own tradition over other traditions like the expansion of Christian missionaries in all parts of the world to enhance the religious capability of Christianity over contemporary religions. On the other hand, Pluralism refers to maintaining a pluralistic nature while adopting cultural trends. For example, a person can be traditional while performing their own rituals of worship and still be modern by respecting all religions or by visiting all forms of religious institutions. It shows a difference or dualism in individual cultural attitudes creating Cultural Differentialism.

Cultural Hybridization

Cultural hybridization refers to the mixing of one or more cultures in a single latitude. It is the most common form of cultural change that takes place with two notions, Cvetkovich and Kellner's *Glocalization* and Ritzer's Creolization. The process of *glocalization* refers to transforming local cultures into global. It doesn't change the previous cultural traits but adds to the basic lifestyle of people. The "Make in India" program launched by the Government of India in 2014 is one such initiative to manifest local sectors to the global level. Indian brands like Royal Enfield, Khadi that are traditional Indian marketing goods are being globalized as a popular form of lifestyle and culture in foreign lands or registration of Darjeeling tea, Assamese *Gamosas* and *Muga Silk*, *Banaras Brocades* and *Sarees* in *Geographical Indication (GI) Tag* by WTO, etc. are some good examples of the process of glocalization.

On the other hand, Creolization is the process of interculturation of two divergent cultures and the formation of some new elements. For example: the use of *Chutneys* in the foreign land as a popular element in their cuisines both in its original form and in the form of Sausages. Besides, Peter England, Monte Carlo, Louis Phillipe, Allen Solly, La Opella, Damilion, etc. are some good examples of creolization of Indian brands where a foreign name is chosen for Indian customers, keeping in mind their fascination for foreign brands. Creolization also develops the local prospects but to some extent overpowers the previous cultural attributes. Thus, culture is a dynamic process. All cultural processes are subjected to negotiation and transformation, especially with the concepts of cultural homogenization, cultural differentialism, and cultural hybridization.

The developing and less-developed societies are mainly pluralistic and hierarchical where the concepts of diversified caste, class, and culture can be found throughout its geographical regions. Similarly, the hierarchical system can be witnessed among all these caste divisions, economic classes, and even in a family. While the developing and less-developed countries have still the culture of rural society and its values are traditional, the urban societies are going through a culture of either ongoing modernity or high modernity due to developed infrastructural services, advanced modes of communication, and interconnectedness. The concept of modernity is further complex. Modernity refers to the rational, scientific, and logical reasoning toward a human being, culture, and all other societal issues. It is an integral element of culture as both material and non-material culture depends on the fact that how rational a society is and how they behave toward the modern culture.

Globalization through its widened connectivity and increased mobility of goods, services, and technology has speeded up the flow of modernity though it may vary depending on the cultures of varied countries. Globalization influences modernity straightly and thus creates new forms of structural and cultural institutions in society.

MODERNITY AS A PROCESS OF CULTURAL GLOBALIZATION

Modernity as a cultural concept started to develop in France for the first time. It spread to other countries of Europe, America, and other developing/less-developed countries aftermath. In developing countries, the concept of modernity was taken as modernization, and it was believed as a synonym for adopting Western values, i.e. if we adopt a Western lifestyle then we are modern. To modify its "Euro-centric" dimension, the concept of postmodernization came in the late 80s or 90s, which was also thought of as the speed-up era of globalization. Again, there started a debate between postmodernists who were also known as hyperglobalizers, and Transformationalists like Anthony Giddens, Habermas, David Held, Bauman, etc. who believed that it is not "postmodernism" but rather "late modernity" or "high modernity" and argued that modernity is not over.

Academic thinkers like Anthony Giddens (1996, p. 6) in his book visualize globalization as a generalized process linked to modernity. He argued that "modern society is a post-traditional society." According to him, modernization is not rejecting the traditions completely. He further stated that tradition remains, but it is examined scientifically in globalization. So only that element which is rational in traditionalism becomes part of modernization. It also focuses on the discontinuities of the modern era and on which terms it is different from the traditional ideologies and institutions. The discontinuities of modern society have coped with "the pace of change", "the scope of change", and "the nature of change'.

The pace of change discusses how the traditional society accelerated its motion toward modernism and accordingly the modern era toward post-modernism. It also looks at the cause of change, which is technology. The scope of change states that with the increasing use of technology, the interconnectedness and social transformation of society are speeding up. Societies are slowly molding toward homogenization and as a result, the earth's surface is becoming a virtual world. The nature of change, however, concerns the changing nature of the institutions. For instance, with modernity, the nature of the political systems of the world regions is changing. With globalization, nation-states are gradually converting into a system of global governance.

Habermas and Blazek (1987) in his book also argues in support of late modernity and states that "Modernity is an unfinished project." Bauman (1999) argues postmodernity as "Liquid Modernity" and states that there is no single description or argument for modernity or globalization. It is a knowledge, ideology, or science to understand rationality and an explanation that reflects the actual world. Hence, he termed it as "Reflexive Modernity." McClelland (1961) felt that the "prevalence of individuals with the psychological trait of high 'need for achievement' was the key to entrepreneurial activity and modernization of society". Hence as the concepts of modernity and traditionalism are not static but change with time hence along with it social structures and culture also change, and it proves that modernity is also a cultural phenomenon that is highly driven by globalization and with the rise of communication technologies, the globalization of culture also gets swift.

COMMUNICATION AND CULTURAL CHANGE

Pye (1963, p. 24) considered mass media communication "an important vehicle of modernity as it is an integral part of the modern communication system". According to Shultz (1993, p. 1) "media create and reflect culture, back and forth, in a rapid process that fuels modernity." By media exposure of a society one can understand the likes and dislikes, living style, attitudes toward one another, cultural settings, etc. that are customary in a social system. It helps people to think toward each other more rationally through the process of interaction and thus diminishes the caste, class, and other socio-demographic barriers among people.

Societies in the world have often faced questions like rich and poor, black, and white, elites and working class, upper or lower caste, etc. since the emergence of the nation. A line of inequality has been prevailing for many ages and communication technologies as an agent reflect this culture and create new ideas and processes leading toward some fundamental changes in the social construction. Mass media through its interactive nature easily transfers the thoughts, ideologies, and beliefs of one community to another more rationally fueling modernity. As a result, community-based organizations, cultural exchange programs, and other media-oriented practices, etc. come to intertwine social inequalities.

The cultural, structural, and societal inequalities changed their forms along with the times but never vanished completely. Communication technologies in this regard act as a mirror-like reflective process to unleash the old and new forms of inequalities present in society and to enhance the levels of modernity in society. Rogers (1962) in his "Diffusion of Innovation theory" argues that the process of communication is linked with the innovation of culture and modernity. As an idea gets innovated it diffuses through various geographical and social boundaries. In this process, the perspectives and behavior of the people toward that idea also change. Those who adopt the newer form modernize and those who do not remain stick to their traditional values. In this way, according to him, the communication processes work to evolve new ideas. He also segmented the receiver of the idea into five categories: (i) Innovators; who invent the idea, (ii) Early Adopters, represent that idea; (iii) Early Majority, the group of commons who accepts the idea favorably; (iv) Late Majority, those who accept the idea depending on the acceptance of majority of people; and (v) Laggards, who never accept the new ideas or conservative. Rogers's theory of development communication also tries to establish the point that how communication is responsible for changing culture.

Along with it the behavior of the society also transformed where people are now engaged in collective or crowd behavior. People in this stage focus on public issues, make a set of morals, and adopt a socially considered identity to build norms and regulations for the mass society. The negative outcomes are misleading social organizations, irrational crowd actions like nonmoral revolutionary mobs and propaganda, etc. Mass media in this sense is a tremendous tool as it can shape the thoughts of society, attach social ties and bonding, and detach social organizations at the same time through its explicit nature of information-bearing.

Here one important point is that with the emergence of new forms of technology, society today is not only limited to material or nonmaterial culture but also familiar with other types of cultural space known as *virtual culture* where people don't know each other physically but they are very known to each other in WEB cloud. This notion of individual-centric society is diminishing the social patterns of joint families encouraging the nuclear type of families as people are more involved with themself rather than everyone, raising the *culture of detachment* and diminishing emotions. Accordingly, the concepts of "social structure influences the culture" and "culture influences the society" have been altered into the concepts of "*technology influences the mass*" and "*mass influences the culture.*" Many significant issues like intellectual property laws, minority-gender, and other socio-political issues, etc. are topics of discussion among the academic group creating a *culture of intellectuals*. Similarly, the safety of women both physically and virtually, their working environment, etc. are creating a *culture of cyber-feminism*. Modern culture is primarily a type of consumer culture, where culture is produced by the demand of the masses or rather can be termed as *the culture of the masses*.

Therefore, the notion of culture is transforming drastically in this era of satellite technology, which makes it inevitable to understand the relationship between globalization and communication to understand the processes of transitions in culture much more elaborately.

GLOBALIZATION AND COMMUNICATION

While some scholars believe that modernity is adopting the Western values and Euro-centric model, others find it is nurturing the rationalities in traditional values also. Due to advancements in communication technology, the process of modernity has sped up in the last three decades of globalization with the globalization of mass media (cable TV and DTH), satellite technology, Internet, and mobile phones and it made it much easier to come in contact with one another's culture and thus adopt the rational ideologies of each culture. Daniel Lerner in this regard is one of the most important critiques of the

Euro-centric model of modernization and finds "empathy" as a way toward actual modernity and he links it with interactive technologies to continue the process of globalization. Daniel Learner's concept of "Empathy" (1958) describes interactive technologies as a way toward modernization. It helps to establish modernization in two ways.

Social Mobilization

It is a way by which society gets inspired to mobilize their home, services, and other infrastructural amenities from one place to another, and communication technologies are a fueling factor for it. It introduces society to their actual needs, emerging needs at a great speed, and as a result the mobilization takes place. For example: people migrate from rural to urban areas in search of better education, employment opportunities, health services, etc.

Empathy or Psychic Mobility

To cope with the living style of the modern world, individuals create a highly empathic capacity, which is the changing cognitive mechanism of a person that inspires them to relocate themselves to another person's position or learn about others' perceptions. Participation in media raises the scope to participate in the welfare of society with a developed learning perception by analyzing the existing factors and helps in establishing modern viewpoints. Thus, learner describes mass media as a multiplier factor for modernization.

Defining the relationship between globalization and communication, McQuail (2006) argues that "the dichotomy of interpersonal and mass media communication has been blurred and people now have access to any part of the globe through new media, based on interactive information and communication technologies such as social media, print media, digital media and so on." Singh (2007) in his paper discusses about global communication system and how it has not only globalized the urban but also the rural areas, especially in a developing country like India. According to him, new communication technologies like "mobile phones have transformed the rural communication systems from a traditional communications system to a modern global communication system. As the elements of traditional/modern/global communication system have been integrated, it resulted into the smooth flow of information even within and outside the village."

Rantanen (2005, p. 4) argues that "most theorists agree that there is practically no globalization without media and communications. It is a process in which worldwide economic, political, cultural, and social relations have become increasingly mediated across time and space". Flew (2007) argues that media have a central place in globalization due to three reasons: firstly, media corporations have increasingly globalized their operations; secondly, the global communication infrastructure facilitates global information flows; and finally, global media play a key role in how we view events across the world in developing shared systems of meaning.

Hence it can be further argued that the development of new communication technologies like the Internet, online advertisement, etc. has helped in the globalization of many product markets. It is creating a cultural dualism of homogenization and digital divide. The nature of globalization is very elastic, similarly, the nature of communication technologies is also flexible. Hence, it becomes very easy for anyone either to adopt or reject the values transmitted over these technologies globally. When any idea is accepted universally and adopted globally, it creates a way for homogenization but simultaneously when there is a dichotomy in any idea it creates an environment of digital divide in the society. Thus, the result is that communication technology impacts the process of globalization enormously and its impacts are diverse for different societies with different cultural values.

CONCLUSION

Globalization in the present time is changing all the dimensions of sociocultural phenomenon. One of the most important changes that it has brought is in the field of communication and culture and the most affected age group that has been affected by it are the youths. A huge population of this young age group is imitating the culture depicted over the Internet and they conceive it as modernity. So, it is a matter of rethinking what is the most impactful concept of modernization and what are its driving tools along with how it is adopted by society. Globalization is a process of social change and modernization is a process itself that leads the society to assimilate with other cultural heterogeneities more rationally and scientifically. The communication process, especially the new communication technologies, is playing a huge role in transforming the shape and structure of a society through cultural globalization. Hence, it becomes mandatory for us to understand the concepts of communication to understand the process of cultural globalization more broadly.

3

COMMUNICATION AS A CARRIER OF GLOBALIZATION

Pye's Communications and Political Development (1963) is one of the pioneering theories regarding the communication process and the level of modernity in developing countries. Based on changing modes of communication, the theory classifies the forms of societal processes into three segments: traditional, modern, and transitional models of society. The traditional society, the form of communication system was mainly face-to-face, had a limited volume of messages, was related to personal ties, and lacked a professional mode of communication. In this type of society, the people are less active in the communication process and thus also lack in the development process of the society. In modern communication systems, the messages are meant explicitly for mass, the volume of messages is huge, and the communication system is much more professional and twofold in nature where systems of feedback are available. Hence this type of society is very active in the development process and is considered in the category of modernized. The majority of the developed and industrialized countries of the world are kept in this model.

The third model of transitional societies is those that are much urban-centric and Westernized in terms of communication modes but belong to a transitional nature. Developing countries like India come under this model where there is a migration from rural to urban areas, people are well connected with the communication system but still prefer to stick with their traditional values, especially in terms of nonmaterial culture. These kinds of societies are both traditional and modernistic depending on the circumstances. Thus, Pye argues about the relationship between the communication process and exposure to modernity in three types of societies in his theory.

Schramm and Roberts (1954) in his models of communication states encoding and decoding a message as the most essential processes of effective communication.

He believes communication is a two-way process and states that until and unless the sender does not receive feedback from the receiver then it is not an effective communication. Thus, he rejected the one-way communication process and introduced the terms "feedback" and "field of experience" in the concepts of communication. His "Field of experience" refers to the values, beliefs, and experience of a person through which perspective he derives the meaning of the message. According to him, the message that is offensive in one custom must be normal for another and hence "field of experience" is an inevitable tool in models of communication.

Berlo (1960) defines the SMCR model of communication, which is also known as Shannon Weaver's Model of Communication. In this model, he argues that the communication process occurs through four different strata, i.e. (i) the sender, (ii) the message, (iii) the channel, and (iv) the receiver. According to him while the previous two are built for the encoding process, the latter two are involved in the decoding process. In other words, a sender encodes a message and sends it by a channel through which the receiver decodes it. In the mean process, many other aspects like the attitude of the sender and receiver, their social system, culture, etc. include the process of communication. McQuail (1969) in the book describes that the process of communication can affect society on two basic levels, i.e. (i) at an individual level and (ii) at a mass level. At the individual level, it changes the methodologies and living styles of an individual primarily, while at a mass level its consequences can be seen in "Mass society, Mass culture and Mass behavior". According to him, these three are the only ideas upon which modern society revolves around. With the term "Mass" he tries to depict the behavior of an institution or structure in aggregate. Mass culture refers to a popular range of activities that a society wants to engage in and respond to collectively raising the question of mass behavior.

Thus, communication is one of the basic processes in a given society. It helps in the organization and operationalization of every society from primitive to the more complex modern industrial societies. For example: primitive and traditional societies have a traditional communication system intermingled with other institutions of the society and have no specific structural units and communicators. However, the process of communication provides stability to the social structure and culture of these societies. In this way, these societies have a specific form of media known as traditional media or folk media, which help in maintaining their traditional culture and traditional form of the society. As society is not static but dynamic, the form of society and culture changes with time. As a result, the communication system of society is also transformed into a new type. In modern society, the communication system is also modern, characterized by specific mass media organizations that produce a "mass culture" or what is called "popular culture," and society is also transformed into a "mass society."

MODELS OF COMMUNICATION

In the study of Development Communications, some important models describe the process of communication. The earliest among them is Aristotle's model of communication, which focused on the role of "*speaker.*" According to it, the speaker plays the most important role in communication as it influences his listeners. Aristotle's model was given in prospect to face-to-face communication for public gatherings like meetings, seminars and conferences, lectures, etc. With the rise of mediated technology, the works on models of communication also developed and some new models came into existence. The most important among them are:

Shannon–Weaver Model of Communication

This model of communication is one of the most simplistic and one of the earliest models in communication studies. This model works upon three columns, i.e., sender, channel, and receiver. It can be understood by the following Fig. 2.

Fig. 2. Analysis of Shannon–Weaver Model of Communication.

According to it a sender encodes a message and passes it through a channel. The receiver decodes it and thus a communication process works. In other words, it is based on one-way communication, which is also criticized by the after-math development communication scholars due to its absence of response from the receiver. In this model, the media technologies like print media like newspapers, magazines, or broadcast media Radio are more relevant.

Schramm's Model of Development Communication (1954)

This model of development communication is the modified version of Shannon–Weaver's model. Schramm denies the model of Shannon–Weaver as he believed that communication cannot be one-way, and the receiver plays a very important role in this through his feedback. Hence, he added two new concepts of "feedback" and "field of experience" in Shannon's model. Fig. 3 represents the same.

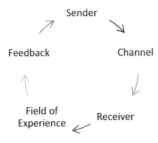

Fig. 3. Analysis of Schramm's Model of Development Communication.

As per Schramm, the way the receiver perceives the message according to his field of experience and the way he gives responses or feedback is one of the most essential components of development communication.

Berlo's Model of Communication or SMCR Model

Berlo's model of communication (1960) also known as the SMCR model includes "sender, message, channel, and receiver" as its components. His model is based on Schramm's model and adds a few more components to it. He defines specifically how "SMCR" works in detail, which can be shown in the following way, as displayed in Fig. 4.

Source/ Sender	Message	Channel	Receiver
Communication Skill	Content	Seeimg	Communication Skills
Attitude	Element	Hearing	Attitude
Knowledge		Touching	Knowledge
Social System	Structure	Smelling	Social System
Culture	Code	Tasting	Culture

Fig. 4. Analysis of Berlo's Model of Communication or SMCR Model.

The model acutely discusses the factors that work behind in completion of a communication process and believes that all the components like our communication, skill, attitude, knowledge, social system, and culture play an essential role in encoding and decoding the message. Besides, it also narrates that the contents/elements, structure, and coding of the message are perceived by the channel through seeing, hearing, touching, smelling, and tasting. This is how a communication process works. Thus, these are some of the most important models in communication studies that describe the most basic processes in the conduct of communication.

MAJOR WORKS/TRENDS IN COMMUNICATION STUDIES

The different forms of media in communication studies have caught the attention of scholars of development communication from the very beginning. Especially the popularity of mass culture, which is also known as Culture *for Commons,* created a bridge between the trends of early and new communication studies. While the previous trends of cultural and communication studies were mainly based on the essentials of living, the new trend was focused more on the sociocultural behavior and lifestyle of the people. This makes it obligatory to peep into the methods of communication research over the periods of two separate times. For a better outlook, the portion has been further divided into two major time zones: trends of early communication research until 2010 and trends of new communication research from 2010 onwards.

Trends of Early Communication Research

The media or technological developments have played a very important role in the creation of a "mass society." Media, due to its wide accessibility and swift nature of mobility created new forms of dependency among people. They now have greater means of control over society and the vulnerabilities of the "real world" can be visualized clearly through media. Thus, the spread of mass media formed a "pseudo-environment" among the mass society where they have increased social control.

It was the period of the 1920s–1950s when the two major fields of concentration of social researchers were: (i) audience research and (ii) its effects on them. In applied research, the interests of the audience play an important role in media production. The behavior, interests, age groups, and their structure were determining factors of the nature of the production of mass culture through mass media. For example, television has seen itself as a leisure resource during this period. The elders and women tended to watch more television due to their leisure interests, whereas the men were more addicted to aggressive programs that were telecasted. Thus, the varying age groups, sex, etc. also played an important role in the production of media content that eventually led to the production of distinctive mass culture.

The structure of audience interests can be both individual and mass in characteristics. In the same way, it can be both positive and negative. Mass media tended to portray crime and violence more speedily, especially in the case of children who are more prone to engage themselves in adult content due to uncontrolled exposure. In many situations, it developed aggressive behavior and undesirable tendencies like anxiety or uncertainty, detachment, estrangement, manipulation, etc. among the audience section.

Thus, media production solely affected the mass society, their opinions, and attitudes, and even interpersonal relations. "Standardization" of society was creating threats to traditional institutions and forming new social and economic prospects. It isolates the individuals from their locales and reinforces material needs over social needs. For instance, people preferred to use media for communication, entertainment, etc. more than interactions with neighbors or community members,. Rather it was eradicating the folk or traditional culture and was creating a homogenized society that has their common nature of taste and societal behavior. Mass media hence forged its direct implications on its audience group as it not only manipulates individual interests but also produces new types of cultural elements based on the selection of media content.

The period of the early 60s to the late 80s witnessed a paradigm shift in the structure of mass society and mass culture. It was a period when the interests of the media producers were shifted from audience research to three specific objectives, i.e., agriculture, health, and education. The media was changing the "state of mind" of the masses and was pushing them toward "modernity." The media users were now encouraged to adopt new technology and practices in the aforementioned fields.

The process of globalization has shrunk the contemporary world into a global village at a faster rate. This has induced a transnational flow of people, objects, and ideas around the globe. Society began to adopt new forms of cultural elements. The two key factors that helped in the development of "mass culture" and "mass behavior" were: "the rise of technology" and "knowledge." The term "mass' here depicted a particular type of structure, behavior, and institution. The major historical characteristics that gave rise to it were the political struggles during the 19th century. The common people used to gather at a certain place and at the same time they used to behave in a certain way in a similar nature. It also created a concept of "totalitarianism" where the people in "aggregate" had "mass character."

The period of industrialization and urbanization also evidenced the pressures of population growth. The agricultural communities were now converting into commercial communities. It governed rapid social change by building new social relationships in the workplace. The idea of "unit" was more clearly visible. *The rediscovery of the community* was going on. Societies were divided into two types: (i) the inherited societies with old traditions and (ii) the emerging societies with new social/market relationships. The feature of this society was the evolution of "mass culture." It referred to a wide range of popularity, access, and active engagement in "mass production" and "dissemination" of culture. The impact of mass culture was mainly seen among the urban middle-class and working-class people. They formed a new kind of culture that included a whole range of popular activities and artifacts. It was in terms of food, painting, cinema, music, and all other aspects of life. It was mainly inspired by emerging social factors like feminism, poverty, anti-racialism, etc., and was later known as "Popular culture."

The development of popular culture further occurred due to three main elements: (i) the spread of literacy, (ii) an increase in personal income, and (iii) leisure. As all three factors were elements of sophisticated and cosmopolitan culture, they differentiated themselves from traditional mass society. It created a sense of "anti-culturalism" among the other groups of society. It forced them to get organized and form new types of cultural artifacts that are more easily communicable, and one can engage themselves with it at a faster level. Mass culture is the one that breaks down all old cultural barriers of class, tradition, and tastes and mixes and scrambles everything together to produce a "homogenized culture."

Trends of New Communication Research

With the development of techno-freak and cosmopolitan cultures, a new trend in communication research has developed. Mass media communication has become an important process in modern industrial societies. Consequently, scholars of communication studies focused on various aspects of communication processes and investigated the relationship between media, culture, and society. The following study aims to analyze the emerging trends of research in the field of culture and communication studies in the last decade (2010–2019) focusing on the research papers published in one of the leading journals in the field of communication studies, namely, *Media, Culture and Society, Sage Publications*. Some of the major vogues in the aforementioned decade were:

Cultural Globalization and Multiculturalism

The study of the relationship between entrepreneurship and popular culture is a major focus of globalization and communication studies. It commodifies popular culture by the process of market expansion, encourages a wave of regionalization like Asian, African, or Western, etc., and creates a new image or vision for the native region in front of the rest of the world. One of the basic focuses in this field is the study of intercultural communication like acculturation, and cultural *"others,"* etc. that are influenced by cultural hybridization. This type of culture is popularized by the mixing of two different cultural elements or is transnational by approach. It is extracted from different local traditions and hence produces a global market for regional cultural commodities. These culturally concerned processes of development generate the concept of "collective conscience" among the specific regions. The recent trends of "boycott Chinese products" and "go vocal for local" in India are some examples that show the concerns of Indian society toward the aggressive economic-cultural policies of China and various *cultural others*. It also focuses on the mapping of cultural landscapes and creates a cultural intimacy or cultural affinity among the homogenous cultural realm.

Besides this, the notion of cultural mediation is another trending theory among scholars of communication and cultural studies. Mediation hereby refers to a mechanism through which the development of sociocultural functions is embodied. It believes that interpersonal communication is a very affecting measure in the formation of a cultural mediation process in society. Folk Tales, dance-music, and language are some of the fueling factors of it as they are very liquid and change their form very frequently and thus help in the mediation of the cultural elements of the society.

Social Media and Emerging Adults

The current decade has noticed a gradual rise in the use of social media, especially among the youth. It has created a new culture of media consumption with new modes of online marketing, e-literacy through apps, social networking sites, etc. that made it compulsory for the intellects of communication studies to focus on the role of social media in the lives of emerging youths. The role of media technology in the development of the social and emotional development of youth, especially in this era of consumerist culture, has grown. It has become a mode of public voice and recognition. The world has turned into a competitive market full of gadgets like iPods, cell phones, video games, etc. that attract adolescents toward themselves as the biggest consumers further turning them into a "miniature adult" changing their dressing habits, food consumption, social behavior, etc. It has also created problems like child abuse *sexting* or electronic swapping of sexual texts and images like revenge scams, bullying and shaming, etc., that generated a trend to study the communication problems of youth in this era of globalization.

Another aspect of the study of youths in communication studies is that the Internet has created new invisible audiences and has brought out the concept of online intimacy that can be also termed as "network intimacy" among the youths. The patterns of social relationships are changing among them. The study of the "lonely crowd" caused by *virtual community* is a new trend in this field that is much prior in youths. It examines a society where one can go to a party, transmit songs over earphones, can dance together but still physically lonely. In other terms, they are connected with the entire globe via communication technologies, still, they are physically lonely in a corner of a house disconnecting itself from the physical world. It additionally raises the notion of endangered childhoods suffering from psychological and emotional stress.

Print Media and Its Transformation Into Electronic Formats

The world is facing fast-growing technological innovations day-by-day that are diminishing the role of old forms of media. Print media is also one such type of media that is getting older but the significance of it continues. As a result, it has become a very important trend for the eminent of communication studies to analyze the role of print media both in its original form and its transformative form, i.e., print media into electronic formats. In this regard, some major topics that are catching attention are the survival of disposable literature like pamphlets, leaflets, comic books, photojournalism, etc. Though there are e-books, e-papers, and e—magazines that came into existence, still book publishing, daily newspapers, finance magazines, etc. play an inevitable role in the construction of society. One important aspect of study in this field is the newspaper crisis, i.e., the narrowing of the printing press' space and conditions. All these factors result in the print media converting into electronic media, resulting in a new cultural change in communication studies.

Globalization of Audio-Visual and Broadcast Media

Audio-visual media was limited to a mode of entertainment only but with time its role has changed. Among the scholars of communication studies, there is tension whether the media is becoming a new mode of innovation or is leading toward discontinuance. It has come out as a mode of nation branding through trendy dramas that create a craze or mania for consumer markets of commodities through regional exports and thus develop economic competitiveness in a region. It creates a worldwide audience, especially for the local cultures of a nation. It is a mechanism for cultural revolution and cultural pluralism in the society. Besides, the study of the *independent television production sector* has come into practice as this sector provides opportunities to work as television workers and thus builds career and network relationships in society. It also studies the job role and emotional, economic, and psychological aspects of these media workers.

The ideological and affective role of audio-visual media in increasing the potential for educational enthusiasm and creating awareness about different societal issues through its programs like through live media events has also been acknowledged. Cinema as a mode of cultural production has gained popularity in the study of culture and communication. For example, cinema makers today are interested in historical and patriotic films creating a notion of national identity building as an objective of film policy. It also creates a question of the hegemony of soft powers and ontological security through television and cinema. Apart from this, broadcast and audio-visual media sometimes unintentionally create an environment of racism, communism, etc. like distinguishing between black and white skin tones in fairness and other types of advertisements and promotions. Hence, the study of *egalitarianism*, i.e., believing all people are equal has been introduced in this field and should be promoted highly.

Among the scholars of communication studies, Gerontology has emerged as a very interesting topic, especially for audio-visual media. Technological innovations have shifted the number of youths toward new media as a result of which the primary viewers of audio-visual media have been shrieked to middle-aged adults and household women. It opened a new scope to analyze the trend of audio-visual media. For the youth, the most interesting programs are reality shows, dating shows, etc., that introduce a new tradition of popular culture. It further creates a scope to study the media audience.

Internet, Online Interactions, and its Discourses

The Internet has become a part and parcel of the recent world. It does not only work as a medium of communication but also plays a major role in the construction of society. Henceforth, the recent scholars of communication study have shifted their interest toward the structural model of technology. This model refers to analyzing the role of humans in producing, designing, organizing, and shaping the contents and practices on the web. Online advertisements, Google ads ,etc., are creating new scope for online communication and business for the local level organizations. Besides, it looks into the fact that how Internet can structure and reflect the issues of society and create a developmental social movement through online engagement and virtual activism. Social websites like YouTube and Facebook are creating a hybrid participatory culture among many interfaces.

Besides this, the digital divide has emerged as one of the most important topics of communication studies. This new trend of study identifies those who are digitally more advanced and those who are behind. It analyzes the factors, reasons, and consequences behind this digital gap in the society. The pros and cons of online interactions are trends in communication research. Though online interactions can create excellent results in the processing of a new thought, the increasing rate of bullying and rage in terms of caste, class, color, etc. in online threads are a new concern for the virtual community.

The case study of *online anonymity* is another factor that is trending in recent communication research. It questions the viability of digital personalities, privacy issues, and illegal occupancies over the Internet. Thus, Internet interactivity and intimacy, Internet negotiation and control, Internet activism and propaganda, and Internet identities and fragilities are some recent cultures of contemporary studies.

TYPES OF COMMUNICATION

Based on the modes of communication, it has been mainly divided into two types:

Face-to-Face Communication

As the name suggests, it is the most simplistic form of communication that occurs between two people or among a group who are engaged in the communication process physically and are known as face-to-face communication. In this type of

40 Globalization and the Transitional Cultures

communication, the communicator doesn't use any forms of media or technology.

Mediated Communication (Include Lucien Pye's Traditional/Print, Modern/Audio-Visual and Broadcasting and Transitional Modes of Communication/New Media)

Mass media refers to a medium through which a string of horizontal connections can be established among the masses or the whole population. The nature of media in the development of society is not static and has been refined since earlier times. Mass media prepare, instigate, and undersign the development of a modern society. The traditional nature of mass media was limited to establishing communication among different people surrounded for a specific purpose like either to provide information of a political order by the ruler or for a commercial purpose with drums, letters, etc. But over time, it became a vehicle to proliferate modernity in the society.

The development of communication technologies like Broadcast media, Television, etc. started to connect people and provide them with knowledge about the entire world. The nature of media was not only restricted to communication now, but it also became a mode of leisure and entertainment. A good number of radios, cinema talkies, videos, and other kinds of discs were available for information and relaxation. The Chicago School of Sociology, which plays an important role in the scientific investigation of communication studies, argues that the role of mass media has been emphasized in the social life of common people. Lynd and Lynd's (1929, 1937) classic studies of "Middletown" depict communication media and leisure as having a great impact on the patterns of everyday life of people, and thus media institutions have become a part and parcel of a larger societal process.

However, a major change took place in the field of communication with the development of satellite communications. The most important characteristic of it was that it carried the features of both interpersonal communication and mass communication. One can use the new media for own interpersonal communication through Facebook, WhatsApp, etc., and for information and entertainment on mobile applications like Jio TV, Hotstar, Twitter, Netflix, etc. The traditional mode of society that was much involved with each other in the real world is transforming into a virtual mode of society today. Its speed, easy accessibility, and instant mode of communication process have made it universally acceptable throughout the world irrespective of religion, caste, and class.

The advancement in communication technologies at the same time transformed mass media communication, which resulted in the integration of various mass media formats into a new form called multimedia. The development of mass media can be mainly divided into three major forms, i.e. traditional media, modern mass media, and new media also known as social media.

Traditional Media

The traditional forms of media as the name suggests include the conventional methods of communication. The primary instruments were the use of drums, smoke signals, puppet shows, letters, folk tales, folk songs, etc., which were mainly perishable types of communication. This kind of media often included oral communication or sometimes just a piece of information that didn't have any written form during early times but lasted for a long period from generation to generation orally. The notable feature of this type of media is that it is transitional. It does not vanish with time but renews itself with the help of modern forms of communication. For example, epics like the Ramayana, The Mahabharata, etc. were mainly oral in their primitive form but with the development of technology, they took the form of "Print media".

Print media refers to all printed materials like newspapers, magazines, posters, pamphlets, etc. The most important feature of print media is low-cost, effective, and easily available to all households and thus highly cosmopolitan. Another feature of print media is that among all traditional and modern mass media technologies, it is the only medium that never gets outdated. For example, newspapers have always acted as a part and parcel with the morning and evening tea for the information-loving society and magazines alike provide all sources of information including films, sports, science, and technology, etc. for both intellectual society and leisure time activity.

The printing and visualization of folk tales like Jataka tales on television, the recording of folk songs, or the printing of the Bible in metal form by Johann Gutenberg in 1455 for the first time are some instances that show though traditional media is still perishable; still, it can't be easily destroyed due to its transitional and quick adaptable nature. Besides, it carries the older cultural traits in modern society regenerating the scope for the process of glocalization.

Thus, print/traditional media over the ages have been maintaining a high level of exposure, especially among the middle-class society to remain intact with the outside world. Though the invention of other technologies like the

42   Globalization and the Transitional Cultures

broadcast radio, television, and cinema, new communication technologies, etc. have tried to become a substitute for it in the later ages; however, print media have always remained a complementary mode of communication irrespective of all classes and generations.

Modern Mass Media

Modern mass media was the successor of traditional media. The most important change in this type of media was the invention of the *Semaphore Telegraph* and *Shutter Telegraph* in 1790s for long-distance communication of the Royal Navy's of Britain. These devices were mainly optical forms of telegraph that worked with the help of towers and visual signals and were the predecessor of the electric telegraph, which was later invented in 1840 and can also be denominated as the origin of imperishable mediums of electrical communication systems. The notable development of modern mass media was witnessed with the invention of the electromagnetic telephone for the first time in 1876. People for the first time exhibit a new world where they can communicate with their dear ones in a much easier and more accessible way.

The invention of broadcast media, i.e., radio in 1890 pioneered the process of filling the information and communication gap among the general public across the world and with time, it saw many other developments in this field. Based on these changing dimensions, modern mass media can be classified into two broad segments, i.e., broadcast media and audio-visual media.

Broadcast Media. The broadcast media comprises media communication systems like radio, podcasts, etc. But radio served as the most important electronic tool for broadcasting technology for its far-reaching audience. The first radio telephony transmission of Fessenden's Christmas Eve from Brant Rock to Massachusetts in the USA in 1906 was the beginning of the reign of radio communication that later became an intrinsic technology during World War I and II after the announcement to censor messages received via radio by the US President Woodrow Wilson for the US Navy in 1914. The British Broadcasting Radio (BBC) made radio technology a public forum in 1923 for the first time by airing a debate on communism. After that the private ownership of radio continued till today.

In India, with the help of BBC in 1957 the All India Radio (AIR) was established, which later came to be known as *Akashvani*, and became the largest technology to provide information, exploring views and ideas of the nation. In 1995 for the first time, private ownership of FM radio started in

India, which remains a good time for the public during their leisure. The popularity can be seen in public transport where the only source of entertainment for both the vehicle drivers and the traveler is to listen to the FM radio channels. The major reason behind the success of radio technology was its suitability to reach unreachable areas, its low cost and easy-to-carry nature, its medium to provide knowledge and information, and its cosmopolite approach. The major examples can be perceived in the high-speed wind and glacier region of Siachen where radio signal emitter programs like "search and rescue" are a great help for the army and militaries for their survival.

Though the radio is still in use among the present generation, its popularity has declined with the development of other modern communication systems like audio-visual media.

Audio-Visual Media. Audio-visual media in modern mass media mainly includes television and cinema. It is audience-friendly in nature due to its stimulus way to connect and exhibit the occurrence of events that are ongoing throughout the world through both sound and picture effects, making the previous method of radio communication less effective among the users. It can telecast to a much wider range and spread the ideas to a wider community, especially due to its average costs of sets. Though initially, it had less impact on rural areas over time it stretched its communication system irrespective of rural and urban setup and is still a favorite pastime and an effective system of mass awareness for the spectators.

In India, it started its journey with *Doordarshan* in 1965, and with the telecast of Asian games in 1982; the production of colored television was introduced. Earlier it was primarily based on one-way communication but with the development of technology, it converted into a source of two-way communication where people can both watch and give feedback and reviews on a specific program as per the need of the hour through talk shows, SMS services and text messaging, etc. Cinema, on the other hand, though a popular pastime irrespective of all generations, the concept of cinema-going is very popular among the youth. But as cable television and satellite channels that are linked through dish antennas are a popular technology to telecast cinemas, the frequency of cinema-going has been relatively declined especially among the middle-class population. The emergence of new media and the availability of all types of entertainment content there like Netflix, Amazon Prime, Hotstar, etc. plays an important role in reducing the popularity of modern mass communication technologies.

Social Media or New Communication Technologies

Social media can be defined as a two-way system of communication where people interact with each other and produce and consume new forms of thoughts and knowledge over Internet-based resources. It emerged with the World Wide Web or WEB 1.0 which was mainly a Read Only Web, but the major development in this category occurred with the arrival of WEB 2.0 technology which was the second generation of web technology and was different from its first generation, i.e., WEB 1.0 in many terms. The major distinction between them was that the first-generation technology was mainly prebuilt and consisted of some static pages from the file server system, but WEB 2.0 produced an opportunity for the flow of information through user-generated content.

With its emergence many new dynamic contents developed over the Internet like social networking sites like Twitter, Facebook, and WhatsApp; user-generated content like wikis, blogging, tagging, etc. and many other application tools. This newly evolved technology not only changed the dynamics of communication systems but also impacted the thought process of human beings as they were now more frequent to day-to-day information and had the power to express their own opinions over a broad platform. At the educational level, it is creating a change through digital media literacy and the use of ICT (Information and Communication Technology).

The application of online tools like cloud computing and big data analytics through primary data collection over the internet is helping educational organizations to know the demographic background, academic interests, and performance of their students, which leads to the betterment of the institution immensely. Besides, social media have been beneficial for many aspects of the society, for instance:

- Social media gives access to knowledge and the right to freedom (especially freedom of speech) at a global level.

- It strengthens the democracy of society through the homogenization of a thought process.

- It provides a platform for public opinions on specific media events along with different political, economic, cultural, and social issues and thus produces new thoughts and intelligentsia among the common citizens declining the class hegemony system of the previous world.

- It provides an outlook on the most trending events and narratives that further help policymakers in their decision-making process to formulate new policies and strategies.

- Social networking sites like LinkedIn, Academia, etc. have created many educational learning communities and employment opportunities through the Internet.

- It reduces the time and cost of data as it is now much easier to reach people across the world and collect data in a shorter period over the Internet.

Thus, social media in the recent world is creating a revolution in every dimension of societal processes. It has become a fundamental need of society to remain informed of their surroundings and WEB 2.0 technologies help in creating that collaborative space to acquaint with each other.

One of the changing facts in this dimension is that the use of WEB 3.0 is already in existence, and it is also known as the semantic web that has been developed in keeping in mind the Web utilization and Web Interaction among the users so that web information can be easily converted into databases for further use. The buzz of artificial intelligence in technological and scholarly society is one of the finest examples of it where WEB 3.0 can distinguish between human beings and robots very clearly and thus provide information according to the utilization. It is gradually transforming from a communication system to a "popular culture" especially among the youth so that they can remain connected with the rest of the world. The popularity of online games like PUBG among the youths is one such example where WEB 3.0 converts the two-dimensional data of WEB 2.0 to three-dimensional data. The only disadvantage of WEB 3.0 is that it is not accessible to all technological devices till now and the devices with less technological advancement may not support the advanced system of WEB 3.0. Thus, communication technologies with their highly advanced form are now creating a revolution in society in terms of both information and communication. Further, through production of knowledge-based workers has been adding intellectual capital to society.

Hence, it can be said that social processes like economy, technological advancements, etc., and culture are inseparable parts of each other, and as the social structure develops, the culture also develops accordingly. As the development of communication occurred, many other processes within it led to the transformation of culture. Hence, the processes of culture that are impacted by the globalization of communication should be studied with a more elaborated method, especially in the case of the global south, where the processes of globalization were always prevalent; however, terminologies like globalization and communication as a carrier of cultural change were a late process. The following chapter will hence discuss the transitions of the communication revolution and its role in cultural change in the global south.

4

TRANSITION IN COMMUNICATION AND CULTURAL CHANGE IN GLOBAL SOUTH

The development of the globalization process speeded up with the development of society and culture. As stated before, the development of agricultural folk society led to the development of traditional culture; the development of commercialization and rural society led to the development of industrialization and modern culture; and the development of industrialization, urbanization, and information society led to the global culture. Hence, it can be argued that globalization, social structure, and cultural structure are interrelated to each other (Singh, 2004). The cultural changes that occur due to globalization have different outcomes for different societies. Brown (1999) argues that "the core values of Western societies, especially as embodied in a culture that places its primary concern on the rights of the individual, are in conflict with the core values of many developing countries. Many cultures in developing countries are based on a concept of protecting the livelihood of ethnic, racial, religious groups, or those who share a common language - not individuals." However, as argued by Jaja (2010), globalization is a natural and inevitable process as no country in the world can avoid or ignore it and failing to embrace it will lead to marginalization. This is why the chapter tries to examine the relationship between globalization, communication, and culture, extensively in the upcoming sections to understand its transitions in the global south.

CULTURAL GLOBALIZATION AND THE GLOBAL SOUTH

Globalization in the contemporary world has changed its nature, form, and shape expeditiously. The concept that emerged with the economic revolution is no longer sticking to it but has spread its roots in political, social, demographic, and cultural elements too in a significant way. Accordingly, its impact is not only limited to economic phenomena but has been transmitted in all other aspects of life. Western traditions especially in developed countries like the US, UK, Germany, etc. globalization is much evident in economic prospects like developing capitalism or profit maximization.

The world has seen the journey of economic globalization from American global footwear production by Nike and the global food industry of McDonald's, Ford as one of the most popular brands of cars among the elites, Suzuki as the biggest car manufacturer for the common public, and China as the largest phone manufacturer, including some of the most famous brands for communication technology like Xiaomi, Huawei, Oppo, etc. that are low budget and common among the general public. All these show a shift in the flow of production from the Western economy to the Asian economy making the latter much more independent, which has only become possible as a result of globalization that made the tariffs and barriers flexible.

During World War II, most of the third-world countries were just recognized as raw material-producing countries and market centers for capitalism. Those countries had their puppet governments established by the colonial forces and had no sustainable economic structure. But after the war, many global organizations like the World Bank, IMF, UN, etc. came into existence that were again controlled by some major superpowers of the world. The third world countries are again considered as less developed or as a periphery by the developed or core countries for their raw materials, land, and cheap labor. New measures were adopted to intervene in the internal affairs of third-world countries with issues like for the sake of human rights, democracy, foreign direct investments, etc. Such methodologies included: war by proxy; for example: Israel is being used by the United States to expand its interest in West Asian countries that are highly enriched with crude oil resources.

But in the developing and global southern countries, the impact of globalization is more cultural. Hence, it becomes important to see how globalization is important in changing the cultural processes. The process of cultural globalization starts with cultural reception. Cultural reception can occur both physically and virtually. For example, in the case of India or the global south, pop culture can be referred to as an element of cultural reception. The emergence of pop songs in South America as a part of anger among the locales is an example of cultural production. When this trend of pop music due to its easy understandability was transmitted to other parts of the world after the development of communication technologies, it became an example of cultural transmission, and finally, its long-way journey from South America to Asia became one of the most popular musical forms with some popular TV shows like MTV Hustle or movies like Gully Boy, Rockstar, etc., especially in countries like India that has its own classical form of music is the finest example of cultural reception.

Due to the growth in communication technologies in recent eras, physical interaction has shifted to virtual interaction; as a result, questions like who, what, why, etc. that create discrimination gradually diminish as in the virtual world anyone can participate in a conversation. Communication technologies through online social activism, television-based programs, etc. have also discarded structural inequalities in society. For example, due to social and audio-visual media, the *LGBTQ* (Lesbian, Gay, Bisexual, Transgender, and Queer or Questioning) community or the community of bisexuals, transgenders, etc. has seen many political, social, and legal reforms in the country. Especially through online activism like spreading the viewpoints of those communities over social media, creating same-gendered dating apps, etc., it has provided them with new organizational freedom to survive among the conservative pattern of traditional societies.

Singh (1986) in his book "Modernization of Indian Tradition" has given some normative variables to analyze the modernization of the society, especially in the case of India which is a part of the global south. According to him "growth of communication" and "media exposure" is one of the key variables to check the level of modernity. For instance, according to him, the modernization of Indian society occurred mainly with Western contact, or when the new Western forms of tradition, culture, education, transportation, and communication processes were introduced. Many types of social reforms like the establishment of Brahmo Samaj and Arya Samaj, the growth of industrial entrepreneurship, and other types of cultural and structural changes were taking place. Mass media in this context not only worked as a tool of information but also as a carrier of modern thoughts and ideologies fastening the process of development. India had some highly modern or advanced scientific knowledge, which we call Indian knowledge systems. Media is also playing a huge role in depicting the same to the entire world.

The land of Rishikesh in Uttarakhand state of India, which is also known as the "yoga capital of the world," witnesses a huge number of visitors throughout the world. In the same manner, Ayurveda, the traditional healing art of India, is so immensely popular among the Western countries that in corporation with the Middlesex University of London, Germany introduced MSc in Ayurvedic Medicine as a professional university degree. The acceptance of Yoga and Ayurveda by the Western communities is one of the finest examples of how traditional substances can be acknowledged as a modern approach among all the communities of society and can be recognized at a global level. All the above works on the relationship between modernity as a cultural element and globalization occurred in either Western or American countries. Hence, it becomes more necessary to understand it as an Eastern value on the global South, especially in a developing country like India.

Many studies count globalization as a threat when comes to the global south. They prefer "regionalization" over "globalization" to keep their cultural elements intact. Ullah and Hannah Ming Yit Ho (2020) in their article "Globalization and Cultures in Southeast Asia: Demise, Fragmentation, Transformation, Global Society" states "With globalization occupying a significant position in both public and private discourses, local culture in Southeast Asia has suffered. Globalization is viewed as a challenge to national culture and sovereignty, South-east Asian nation-states have also responded to globalization by endorsing regionalization. But regionalization is aimed to strengthen ties among its member nations with shared values and goals to preserve their Eastern cultures by learning from one another via a multilateral platform."

Raisa and Tasnim (2020) in "McDonaldization of Asia: Impacts of Globalization on the Asian Culture" studies the impact of McDonaldization in countries like Bangladesh and Malaysia and found that cultures are changing rapidly due to globalization. The causes they mention are to keep appealing to Western tourists. It argues that "culture has seen a downfall. As more Westernization takes place, the newer generation is inclined toward it and deviates from the already diverse local culture." It also creates a distance from social realities especially among the younger generations and deviates them from ethnic elements.

The primary concepts of modernization depict themselves as a Euro-centric or Western notion but as the world stepped into a post–modern era, the concept of modernization changed too. At present modernization doesn't only refer to Western values but it has become a two-way process, where cultures assimilate with one another, reevaluate their pros and cons rationally, and further adopt the value-components of one another according to their perceptions. It doesn't mean discarding the traditional form of values and lifestyle rather it encourages the spread of ethnic traditional elements to the entire globe. Similarly, Hosseini (2010) examines the impact of globalization on Iran and argues that globalization "does not mean simply being a recipient or a provider. We must find areas of collaboration where we can act as partners with different organizations and interact in a mutually beneficial way". Thus, the impact of globalization is complicated in the global south, and it needs to come out as a collaborative approach where the cultural receptions are both local and global. It should recognize all the rational elements of all cultural entities and create a better modern society.

One of the important societies of the global South is the tribal society. The global south comprises the parts of continents like Asia, Africa, and South America, which are the home to the largest sections of indigenous people. According to the United Nations Economic Commission for Latin America and the Caribbean (UN ECLAC), Central and South America and the Caribbean region are home to between 45 and 50 million indigenous people (United Nations Department of Economic and Social Affairs, 2015). While the African continent has the highest number of tribes in the world, India is the largest country with having tribal population. Some of the world's oldest and largest tribes like Gond are inhabitants of India. While these tribes are believed to be a community that resides in the remotest corner of society, they are not much acquainted with modern technologies and live a life based on primary occupations with a low level of literacy and infrastructure. This is the reason why when discussing the processes of globalization and modernity in different societies, it becomes important to understand the impact of it on tribal societies especially when we talk about the global south, which is home to the highest number of tribal populations.

TRIBES IN THE GLOBALIZED CULTURAL PERSPECTIVES

The tribes are one of the largest indigenous groups of the society. They are the original individuals of the soil and the bearers of the ethnicity of the region. Culture and language are the two major ethnic components that distinguish tribes from any other castes and communities. Further, the fact that no castes have their particular language and sociopolitical organization differentiates them from specific tribes, which are more confined to their specific region based on remote/hilly areas and self-autonomy. Since the reachability has increased globally due to the rapid communication revolution, the scope for tribal studies and interest in understanding the tribal communities also grew. According to Bodhi and Jojo (2019), the tribal aspects can be divided into three different viewpoints, i.e., the colonial construct, the postcolonial construct, and the Indigenous people's construct on tribes. While the colonial construct refers to studies of tribes as primitive, barbaric communities, the postcolonial constructs discuss aspects like isolation, assimilation, and integration which still find the irrational and focus on modernizing them. The Indigenous people's construct on the other hand, talks about tribal autonomy, identity, language, and culture, and tries to evolve the community through their preexisting knowledge systems. While the colonial and postcolonial construct on tribes is mainly based on the Western perspectives, the latter, i.e., Indigenous people's construct based on their own perspectives. Hence, the process of understanding tribal lifestyle is not limited only to the global south but the Northern researchers from the US and other European countries like Great Britain also gradually developed an interest in the tribal lifestyles.

One such British scholar is Verrier Elwin who proposed the "Isolation theory" (1939) of the tribes and the first foreigner to become an Indian citizen. He was also a member of the tribal development committee through the Five-Year Plan in 1957. However, the theory proposed to him was not accepted broadly as his ideas were based on Western civilizational ideologies, and based on it, he mentioned the tribes as "Primitive," which was later considered derogatory for a community. He further advocated leaving the tribes "alone" in their place, which cuts them out from mainstream society entirely. Based on it, the concept of "Inner Line Permit," which is an official permit document also notified in Indian states like Arunachal Pradesh, Mizoram, Nagaland, and Manipur, which restricts the movement or mobility of the common people from the protected region. To modify his theory, G. S. Ghurye (1963) gave the "Assimilation Theory" but again it was rejected as he mentioned the Indian tribes as "Backward Hindus." The theory was not acknowledged much as the tribes from any region have their own religion and they are mainly nature-worshippers, hence assimilated into any particular religion. The "*Hinduism*" which they follow is a sister religion and as a part of cultural globalization, it was received as a common religion in most of the Indian tribes. It created a bridge between the two cultures where tribes, due to the elements of nature-worshipping present in Hinduism accepted it with a warm heart.

Further, this process of cultural assimilation was studied acutely by Virginius Xaxa who proposed the "Integration Model" (2014) of tribes. This model was highly appreciated as according to this model, assimilation of culture is good but complete assimilation is a problem because it will create cultural convergence or merge the local culture into the dominant culture. It is based on the concept of "identity articulation" where due to assimilation of cultures, no culture should be converged into another where a small ethnic group loses its own cultural traits. All these models try to understand the impact of cultural globalization on the tribes of the global south, especially India, and how it affects their cultural ethnicities.

If discussed thoroughly, it can be seen that the tribes in these regions are very harmonic and based on the notion of laughter and love for people. In the words of Nelson Mandela, they live on the philosophy of "Ubuntu," which refers to *I exist, and We exist.* The Indigenous philosophical principle visualizes the world rooted in human beings and an indefinite coexistence with nature. They believe in love and to be loved, relation, reciprocity, correspondence, and sustainability. However, due to the domination that the cultural others try to establish in their community and region, they often perceive them as cultural intruders, which is also rational in some cases. One such example is Jarawas of the Andaman Islands. A primary hunter-gatherer group that has had their habitat on the island approximately since 60,000 years ago, were the largest sufferer of various development/modernity-based atrocities. According to Sarkar (1990), the Jarawas were discovered by the British during the first penal settlement in Colebrooke (1789–90) and Blair (1789–96) where they tried to establish the outsiders in middle Andaman, which was the homeland of Jarawas. It impacted their privacy, ethnicity, and harmony at a large due to which during the second penal settlement (1858–1946) they protested and became hostile to safeguard themselves. The situation has not developed ever since then and till now they prefer to remain separate from any outsiders or their cultural domination.

Thus, globalization when studied deeply can have both positive and negative impacts on the cultural ethnicities. In most of the cases of tribes, they have their negative impacts. Further, if the colonial past is studied, there are numerous examples where the tribal people from the entire global south have faced the atrocities sometimes due to their color or sometimes in the form of slavery. These cultural elements especially can be observed in various names given by the outsiders for the tribal groups of the global south like "Red Indians," which is a very offensive word for a native American. Similarly, in India, if one sees the Bonda tribal group of Odisha, they call themselves as "Remo" meaning hilly people. But as they came into contact with the cultural others, they were popularized with the name "Bonda," which refers to semi-naked, which was highly derogatory.

Besides, there are also various tribes who due to cultural homogenization have lost their cultural elements completely. One such example is the Meena tribe of Rajasthan. The tribe due to its location has seen cultural assimilation with mainstream societies of the country. They have been inclined toward a high level of education, job roles, and information technology. But in the meantime, they have also adopted the mainstream cultural entities, religious practices, and other elements like clothing, food habits, etc., and left their cultural ethnicity completely creating a threat to their cultural survival. Thus, the impact of cultural globalization is high among the tribes. In some cases, it helps them rationalize themselves with education, health, communication technologies, and other infrastructural facilities, on the other hand sometimes it becomes a challenge for the tribes to retain their cultural traits. However, one continuous element occurring in the tribal communities due to the impact of globalization is their cultural transition. This suggests a separate study for globalization and its impact on the cultures of the tribal communities especially in the global southern countries.

CONCLUSION

Thus, globalization is a multifaced phenomenon that has diverse results in different communities and different regions. According to Cruz-Saco (2018), "globalization centers around the need to eliminate the urban/rural gaps, equalize access to social services, and enhance living conditions of indigenous people who live in poverty. In the case of women also a paradox has emerged: although indigenous women have displayed significant activism, they carry the greater burden from their double duty of working outside the home and providing care at home." It indicates the fact that globalization in some cases is encouraging modernity, whereas sometimes it also creates negative cultural hegemonies.

The concepts of globalization and modernity are an integral part of each other and without studying the level of modernity in society the level of globalization and its impact can't be studied individually. At the same time, contemporary ideas and discourses of development are also undergoing through process of intellectual debates and analysis creating academic dissents among the scholars. Impact of forces of globalization and communication technological advancements (together) on the process of cultural change (level of modernity) on different sections of society exposed to these new communication technologies as these communication technologies facilitate instant global communication. They are part and parcel of the globalization process (economic, political, cultural, environmental). Hence, it raises one of the basic questions:

Whether in societies like India is there any change in the level of modernity and culture as a result of globalization and digitalization?

In the question mentioned above, the rigidity of norms and values tightens up for marginalized sections like tribes, women, and middle-class groups of society. Hence to understand the level of modernity in value-based countries like India it becomes necessary to understand the status and dignity of these sections with special reference to such countries. Recognition of pluralities of life, and understanding the indigenous knowledge systems, and cultures can create a real magnitude of development and a more rational or modern society, and forgetting it can result in epistemic injustice causing a negative globalization. The above sections of the chapter have already discussed the tribal society and its relationship with globalization and modernity. The studies also establish the fact that globalization affects the gendered aspects of society separately. To follow this up, the next chapter will take the study of women as a marginal section of society and will do a detailed study, especially taking India as its study area to understand the Eastern perspectives of globalization on them.

5

CULTURAL GLOBALIZATION AND THE MARGINAL PEOPLE: THE CASE OF INDIA

OVERVIEW

Women are always considered as the marginal sections of society, throughout the world. In the case of India also, the story is not different. Indian society is mainly formed based on the concepts of caste and patriarchy due to which the women become marginalized. Various socioreligious norms and complex ties of society may lead tribes and women to lack proper representation in society. Concerning it, the chapter tries to understand whether cultural globalization as a liquid process has helped to change the situation of the marginal sections in society. The world is moving toward digitalization and social media as a form of new media can shape the thinking process of the human mind in the way it wants. Many female-oriented movements were occurring frequently over these platforms that can somehow reshape the condition of women in society through the globalization of thoughts and culture. Hence, keeping in mind all such minute but important aspects, the present paper tries to understand the aspects of women in the cultural context of India.

WOMEN AND MODERN CULTURES: AN EMPIRICAL STUDY

The Indian society is patriarchal. Not only India but if one wanders in any part of the world, they will observe the numbers of men larger than women in every sphere of life. The ratio is always high, as a result of which it always happens that from one generation to another the preexisting male-dominating foundations proliferate. These become one of the main reasons that curtains down the role of women in society from being perceptible and gradually it makes the male dominion upsurge in comparison to females. The societies in this way start to move on from the rules made by males and females finally become the second gender. Their contributions become discreet in front of contemporary society and as an outcome, the questions like the role of women and discussions on the topics like women empowerment arise.

The concept of feminism is nothing more than a challenge to the established dominance of patriarchal society. It is a concept that carries nothing new in terms of understanding but it is a visual of our day-to-day life through which our women are fighting with. In their everyday life, they face various good or bad experiences. While those good experiences can be termed as empowerment of women, the bad experiences can be quoted as miseries of womanhood. The broad literature on feminism is mainly divided into three schools: Liberal feminism, Radical feminism, and Social/Marxist feminism (Allen, 2021). In all of these schools, power plays a significant role. In the larger picture of society, power is a very dynamic term. It can both construct and destroy any individual, organization, or society as a whole. Arendt (1958, p. 200) defines it as "power springs up between men when they act together and vanishes the moment they disperse". Liberal feminists believe power is a resource to distinguish among the genders (Allen, 2021). Liberal feminist like Susan Moller Okin argues that the modern gender-structured family unjustly distributes the benefits and burdens of familial life among husbands and wives (Allen, 2021). Okin further argues "When we look seriously at the distribution between husbands and wives in terms of work (paid and unpaid), power, prestige, self-esteem, opportunities for self-development, and both physical and economic security, we find socially constructed inequalities between them, right down the list" (Okin, 1989, p. 136). In the same way, radical feminists believe power is domination (Allen, 2021).

These schools concentrate much on adversities in relation to women like patriarchy, exploitation, violence, and oppression of women. It talks about the behavioral approach toward women done by men and scholars like Young (1990, p. 155) argue "At the root of those modalities, is the fact that the woman lives her body as an object as well as subject. The source of this is that patriarchal society defines woman as object, as a mere body." The third school of social feminism sees power as a tool of capitalism. According to them in gendered issues also "women were becoming the new face of the international proletariat" (Fernandez-Kelly 2007, p. 509). According to Armstrong (2020), "Women's subordination was neither biologically natural nor God-given; instead, the class relations of capitalism enforced the gender hierarchies that anchored women's oppression". Though all the school raises different issues on women still their focus remains on the development of women. The common factor here is that all the schools talk about dependency. It indicates underdevelopment. The dependency of women on men for socioeconomic limits fuels concepts like oppression or domination. In this regard, education is the only pathway that can lead women to be strengthened both socially and economically further unknotting the threads of dependency.

In India, the women in our daily interactions are considered inferior most of the time. This is mainly due to their biological structure and stature. They often come face to face with issues like domestic violence or misbehavior from time to time till now. The instances are much apparent among poor women. Because even if they go through any such misdeeds, still either due to the power of the elite community or due to the fear that they will lose their only way of earning, they remain silent. In this way, most of the cases remain unnoticed. Hence until the women are encouraged to gather themselves and speak out with a loud voice the question of feminism or women empowerment will not solve. Societal norms and preexisting culture of male dominion are also a cause of it where the women feel that it will be a question of their dignity, both on themselves and their family if they speak about the craps. The scenario is found all over the world and India is also not devoid of it. No discussion or forum can solve these issues unless the women on their own take the responsibility to empower themselves. In the Indian scenario, to understand it more clearly one needs to turn out the pages of history and Indian culture, to know the aspects of women in the country.

INDIAN WOMEN THROUGH AGES

The Indus Valley civilization, which evidenced the earliest cities of the Indian subcontinent near 2600 BCE, was purely a matriarchal society. The traces of art and sculptures clearly state the fact that the people of Harappa and Mohenjo-Daro used to worship Mother Nature and the female sculptures were dominant. Though some scholars like Richard Meadow argued that they are not the sculptures of Goddesses still the sculptures clarify the fact that women were an inseparable part of their lives. In the Vedic times, women were not only the backbone of a family but also it was said "The family where women exist, there exists the God." They were given a very prestigious position and often worshipped in the form of a Goddess. The examples can be seen through very religious books and Vedic scriptures where we first found the Goddesses like Parvati, Laxmi, Saraswati, etc. Their divinity is not only

60   Globalization and the Transitional Cultures

described orally but also in daily practices or worship ceremonies they can be observed through the lines from *strotas* (hymns) like,

> *Suravara varshini, durdara darshini, Durmukhamarshani, harsha rathe,*
> *Tribhuvana poshini, Sankara thoshini, Kilbisisha moshini, ghosha rathe,*
> *Jaya Jaya Hey Mahishasura Mardini, Ramya Kapardini Shaila Suthe*
>
> —Mahishasura Mardini Stotram

(**Meaning**: *One, who gives boons to the gods, kills the wicked and is joyful in herself, the nurturer of the three worlds, the one who satisfies Shankar, the one who removes sins and roars fiercely and who is angry with the demons. Hail, Hail to you, the daughter of the mountain, the one who dries up the pride of the egoistic*).

These lines clearly show how strong the women were portrayed at that time and what power they believed to be possessed. Not only the divine forces but many examples of women like Gargi, Maitreyi, Lopamudra, Anusuya, etc. can be mentioned as the scholars of Vedic knowledge at that time. Not only these scholars but also two of the greatest epics of Sanatan Dharma, i.e. the Ramayana and the Mahabharata revolve around women as its center. While in the previous epic Sita, the wife of lord Rama was abducted and to free her, the entire army declares a war, similarly, in the second epic, to do justice to the unjust that happened in the name of womanhood, bore by the queen consort Draupadi, the entire battlefield was bloodshed. The epics indicate the fact that at that time how much the dignity of a woman mattered and how people were conscious about the respect of a woman.

In the medieval period with the arrival of various conquerors, there came a change in the cultural practices. The most affected groups were the women. They were forced to remain under veils to escape from the outsiders, the evils. Patriarchy was at its peak and patriarchal ideas subdued the forms of *Shakti* (Matriarchal powers). The instances of women being treated as the second gender or stopped from being leading the society took place. Though we found very few examples like Razia Sultan, Nur Jahan, Gulbadan Begum, Jahanara Begum, etc. in the pages of medieval history still their numbers are negligible. Another reason that left them behind was that though they had a prominent role whether it was ruling the empire or their contribution in the form of authors of highly rich pieces of literature like Humayun Nama; their roles were limited mainly inside the *Harems* (part of the house where Mughal consorts used to live) or they were quoted as a portrayal of beauty in the poetries or songs. The time of the first independence war the first time emerged women heroes like Laxmi Bai, Jhalkari Bai, Begum Hazrat Mahal, etc. in the pages of Indian history after the Vedic times. Later in the period of the independence war, many female freedom fighters throughout the country emerged as the leaders.

In the period between the 1960s and 1980s, the entire world was going through the first wave of feminism. The issues and concepts of women's empowerment were trending all over the world and people were getting conscious about the rights and freedom of women. But in the Indian scenario, the wave was not very visible. Women in the country used to live their usual lives and engage in household chores. With the emergence of communication technologies, some differences were noticed like people were getting more educated, especially the importance of education for women were encouraged through campaigns like *Beti Bachao, Beti Padhao*. Globalization of media technologies also brought a new change and with the development of social media in today's time like Facebook, Twitter, etc. various online movements like *Me too, Nirbhaya*, etc. came into vogue. Even in political campaigns also the importance of women in Indian society is quite evident.

WOMEN IN CONTEMPORARY INDIA

A lot of debate and talks about women's rights and violence against them have been raised within these years. But in a country like India where women are holding various higher political as well as social positions from being the President of the country to foreign ministers, defense ministers of the country to finance officers and chief ministers; there should not be a debate on women empowerment. In New India, from the largest MNCs of the country like Reliance to banking sectors, from Rafael flight commandants to Olympic medal winners, the role of women is visible. Even if the period of COVID is taken into consideration, still women are the largest group to serve society whether in the form of staff nurses, *ASHA* workers, or COVID testing and vaccination providers. In the village economy also, rural women play a very significant role. All the members of self-help groups in the villages of India are women. They through various handloom activities or other minor activities like doing horticulture/apiculture, making incense sticks or perfumes made out of flowers are contributing to the economy continuously for which they must be praised.

The recent governmental schemes have given special priority to women both in the educational and in job sectors. In National Education Policy, 2020, more than 1000 institutions have been consulted for the inclusive approach and to ensure inclusivity, especially for gender many steps have been already taken. These include residential schools and hostels like Kasturba Gandhi Balika Vidyalayas (KGBVs), provisions for Netaji Subhash Chandra Bose Awasiya Vidyalayas and Hostels, Rani Laxmi Bai Atmaraksha Prashikshan (self-defense training to Girls), Swami Vivekanand Single Girl Child Fellowship for Research in Social Science, PG Indira Gandhi Scholarship for Single Girl Child Stipend for CWSN (Children with Special Needs) girls where 91,318 children with special needs girls covered under home-based education. Similarly, the government is also providing various financial assistance for women's enterprise development and other job-related schemes. These all work as a procedure to strengthen women and their education to make them financially independent. Communication technology plays a very important role here as social media and other mediums of information providers and advertisers can spread knowledge about all these gender-inclusivity schemes to a larger section within less time. It can approach women not only residing in urban areas but those also living in remote corners. It is a two-way process where there is always a scope where foreign companies can invest in those women through various funding and other assistance.

Education and financial independence make women come out of their cultural barriers. They visualize a new world where they are equally important in policy-making, governance, and decision-makers. It develops a sense of equality among them naturally and hence the societal norms also become flexible. Thus, in the contemporary world education and financial independence are coming out as a stereo-breaker that can bring enormous cultural changes and waves of modernity in society, especially among the marginal groups.

THE REMARKS

There is no need to equalize men with women as women pose equal strength to men naturally. The only need of the hour is to support a female in every sphere of life both by the males and females residing in this society. Even in the pious scriptures like the Bible, *Manusmriti*, etc., it is very notable that God created both men and women at the same time whether in the form of *Adam and Eve* or *Manu and Shatarupa*. Actually, in the equalization process of men and women, the woman herself plays a very crucial role in displaying the gender as the feeble one, especially in terms of Indian Society. The mother who gives birth to a new child is responsible for its upbringing and as a mother, her first duty should be to neglect the crown of the second gender and make her daughter understand how she should be socially empowered and how she should behave in the society as a strong woman who can deal with all the adversities of the society. The same goes for the male counterpart. He must teach his son what are the limits and how to behave socially as well as emotionally with all the women in the world. In this way, it is a behavioral interdependence that ultimately turns into sociocultural norms. In terms of Indian society, it is often seen that girl children are always taught how to behave in a society, how to talk in a decent language or dress up properly or how to carry themselves up in a social gathering, how to treat elders but the same does not go for the male counterparts and it is said to be all right for a boy to act in any way he feels comfortable. This is the main reason why the process of equalization is lacking.

The rise of globalized media can be very effective in changing the scenario. Previously it took many days to get any news from one place to another but in today's condition, it is very quick. It takes just a few minutes to spread the news to the nooks and corners of the world. Hence, if any such news claims that violence against women is taking place, for such incidents the only responsible factor is the family members, which are the smallest unit of our society. In various studies conducted on domestic violence, the fact came out that the women, i.e., the women themselves knowingly or unknowingly become a major reason for their oppression and it is due to the prevailing thought that violence against women is nothing new. It occurred previously, it is occurring now, and it will also occur in the future. Hence, one must adapt to this environment and act accordingly. The same ideologies go up from one generation to another and even the children in the house also learn the same from the time of their childhood that the male ill-behaved with their female counterparts but still the women treat them well and hence it becomes a natural process that the son or the male can ill behave and the daughter or the female will bear this ill behavior. Though these trends are diminishing at a good rate, and one can experience the presence of women in all the fields of life like education, politics, sports, culture, etc., hence, the only need of the hour is to give equal education to both sons and daughters.

The role of women in making society can also be related to the three necessities, i.e. food, clothing, and shelter. Women, whether housewives or working remain responsible for providing food to the family, especially in Indian society. If she works outside for the entire day still it remains her utmost concern whether food has been prepared, whether her family had their food properly or not. She also ensures that food is being filled with nutrition and healthiness, which will not be in the street or outside foods. This is also the reason why women are in charge of making food in their household and this factor depends completely on their own will. Nobody forces them to do so. In this sense also women are contributing to nation-building by raising a healthy child or family. This is very important, but the facts always neglected the role that women have played since the evolution of society, and they were never credited for such initiatives that they played for making a country healthier. In terms of shelter also it is often said in Indian context that "A house becomes a home when a female resides in it." She is believed to be the *Laxmi* of the house and is given the position of the goddess who brings prosperity and wealth to the house. The new generation of women is very conscious about the social development of their household. Even a housewife who engages in household chores for the entire day rigorously and comes in the category of unpaid workers who never claim any reward for their sweat due to their motherly nature contributes unconditionally to the development of the house. She ensures that none of her children remain hungry or none of them lack education. They try to ensure the best life they can provide for their children and hence the famous quote of Brigham Young, "You educate a man; you educate a man. you educate a woman; you educate a generation" perfectly fits this situation.

In Indian society, the results are visible in the form of diminishing gaps in the rates of sex ratio. It is a symbol that ancient Indian Vedic culture is re-emerging where women are seen with divinity. They are comparatively conscious of the importance of equal share in both genders. Even in the backward areas where the previous generation women were not so privileged, they are now taking inspiration from the women who have established themselves in dignified positions and are willing to idealize them for their daughters and the upcoming female generation. Hence, it is a very clear scenario that the mothers are the most important unit in developing a society and they are the backbone of a family who can teach their daughters to become strong enough to be able to make their own decisions and know about their rights.

One of the biggest obstacles that existed previously and still exists is the dowry system. It is the biggest evil that forced generation to generation to believe daughters as a burden for the family. But the diminishing rate of it is also a good indicator of the development of a traditional society and in this regard, the new generation of men should be very determined they never demand dowry, nor do they accept it as a token of love. So many women are

Cultural Globalization and the Marginal People 65

still fighting with the adversities of society, they are not very privileged and are often stuck in problems like domestic violence, human trafficking, or misbehaved by men. Hence, we should take steps for them and educate them or show them the right path so that they don't push themselves into such dangers. Education is the only measure in this regard and the new India is continuously developing and the role of women in this regard is very prominent. The target should be making a society where there remains no need to discuss the topic of women's empowerment.

One of the biggest problems here is that the women don't come out to speak for themselves and even if someone tries to speak for them, they become hesitant to talk about their problems such as exploitation, violence, etc. The two major reasons for this is the societal pressure and the second is their emotional psychology. To come out from this problem one must introduce the victims to such personalities who can be ideal for them or from whom they can take inspiration. There are many women like Savitri Bai Phule, the first women teacher of India Pandita Ramabai who is known as the first feminist of modern Indian history, and many organizations like Sampat Pal's *Gulabi Gang* who are continuously fighting for such causes. It will automatically make them think about the mental pressure they are suffering from and show them the way to speak for themselves. In this way, one woman can become ideal for another woman and will play an important role in making a nation with strong women. It mainly revolves around families and educating every member of the family can eradicate this problem. For example, if a father takes care of the rights of her daughter, the sons take care of the rights of their mother, the husband takes care of the rights of their wife, and the brother takes care of the rights of their sister; the problem can be visibly diminished. The same goes for the females also. For instance, if the mother takes care of the rights of her daughter, the daughters take care of the rights of their mother, and the sister takes care of the rights of their sister then also the problem will decrease at a large scale. One should take care of the way they talk or behave in their families about the women or with the women. Because family is the first unit where one learns and from where changes can take place. The changes in this regard are also visible enough. In a country like India even during the last decade, women were treated very delicately, especially in the village areas. They were either accompanied by their brothers or any male members of their family while going to schools or markets but now it has been observed the girls are going to schools or markets on their own sometimes by bicycle or sometimes with peer groups. The changing scenario is an indicator of the fact that the fear of being women is gradually decreasing and females and their families are feeling it safe to accomplish any work by their selves without taking any support from their male family members. In this way, they will be empowered automatically and no question or discussion on women's empowerment will be left in the future.

Youths can play a very important role in diminishing the gaps between the two genders. They are the generations that possess the capacity to adopt the good and discard the evil. They should remain devoid of any pre-determined notion, and this is the reason that can be very helpful in changing societal norms. For example, as a technologically privileged generation, they can compare various cultures and replace the good values of other cultures with the bad ones. They as well-educated people can also alert people over evil acts like teasing a woman or making inappropriate behavior toward them. Through social media also they can force the government to be stricter toward such deeds and help to set up standard norms on behavior toward women. Thus, grassroots-level changes can also help in bringing favorable changes in society, especially in the field of women discourses. It also transforms the level of rationality among societies and disregards the sociocultural taboos that create a negative impact on society. The next chapter will try to assess the levels of rationality, i.e., modernity in Indian society to understand the impact of globalization both in material and nonmaterial culture.

6

GLOBALIZED TECHNOLOGIES AND MODERNITY: AN ASSESSMENT

This chapter is based on quantitative factors to determine the levels of modernity both in material and in nonmaterial culture that have occurred in the recent past due to globalization, especially in the field of communication. As the study tries to examine the effects of globalization on developing and traditional countries like India hence the locality or the area of the study has been identified as different parts of India. A survey was conducted online where almost 1600 respondents were identified as the population of the present study to understand the scenario of the globalization factor. India is a country with heterogeneous caste, class, and races. In a real sense, the proverb "Unity in diversity" is the most important feature of the country and while examining the notion of globalization to understand its effect on middle-class people, especially the youth becomes very crucial. Youths here are important because they are the inheritors of the present, as well as future generations. The youths are the group that has been affected by the communication revolution at its utmost. "Middle Class" is a product of the neoliberal economy that emerged after the 1990s with liberalization and privatization under the New Economic Policy, in 1991 in the country. This New Economic Policy was a turnover for the country as it not only created the concept of a "Neoliberal Economy" but also emerged the notion of "class" in caste-based Indian society. But the most prominent among them was the "middle class". According to the Merriam-Webster dictionary "the middle class refers to a fluid heterogeneous socio-economic grouping composed principally of business and professional people, bureaucrats, and some farmers and skilled workers sharing common social characteristics and values." Hence the age group, sex, religion, mother tongue, caste, marital status, income, languages known, educational level of the respondent, father's education and occupation, mother's education and occupation, native place, length of residence in the city and household consumption pattern etc. has been considered as an important variable in this chapter to justify that the facts revolve around middle-class society itself which is the largest economic class in Indian society as well as to understand their living style regarding the present times. In the same manner the term "youth" is an important criterion in this chapter. Hence, the age groups of the youths are selected based on "National Youth Policy, 2021" that declares the age group of youths from 15 years to 29 years. The chapter will scrutinize the socioeconomic background and the exposure to mass media as a base to understand the changes in the cultural emotions of people taking place due to the globalization of communication. The cultural change will be analyzed in terms of material culture as well as nonmaterial culture (modernity). Material culture includes the style of life of the youth reflected by their patterns of consumption and other aspects of material culture. Nonmaterial culture will be analyzed in terms of their values, societal norms of the society, and their beliefs. To do so based on the responses derived, they will be given rankings based on the Overall Modernity Scale (O.M. Scale) developed by Inkeles and Smith (1974). The scale is measured on five levels and the total score on the scale is 34. The subdivision is like 1. Very low (1–8), 2. Low (9–16), 3. Medium (17–24), 4. High (25–32) and 5. Very High (33–40). For conservatism 0 score is given and for modernity 1 or more is given. Based on this scale, the outcomes will be generated to examine the levels of modernity and ongoing cultural change concerning middle-class youth.

SOCIOECONOMIC BACKGROUND OF THE RESPONDENTS: AN ASSESSMENT FOR MATERIAL CULTURE

(1) The number of respondents in the age group of 20–25 years is relatively high with 45.6% followed by the age group of above 25 years (41.6%). The representation of youths under 20 years is low with 12.8%.

Although, the total number of male and female respondents is the same they differ from each other in terms of their age group. Among the male respondents, the representation of the age group above 25 years is relatively high (45.6%) while among the female respondents, the age group of 20–25 years has relatively high representation with 48.0%.

(2) More than three-fifths of respondents (69.2%) belong to Hinduism; a few more than one-fifth (28.0%) of them profess Islam. The representation of

Globalized Technologies and Modernity: An Assessment 69

the other three religions, namely, Christianity (1.2%), Buddhism (1.2%), and Sikhism (0.4%) is relatively very low. If analyzed gender-wise then the distribution of females is higher in both of the largest religions in the sample, i.e. Hinduism (71.2%) and Islam (28.8%). Among the male respondents, the representation of Hindus (67.2%) and Muslims (27.2%) is relatively low with 67.2% and 27.2% respectively. Among the female respondents, there is no representation of Christians, Sikhs, and Buddhists.

(3) A little more than half (52.8%) of the respondents come from the General category, making the majority of the sample, followed by the Other Backward Categories (OBCs- 32.8%) and Scheduled Castes (SCs- 12.0%) who constitute about one-third and one-tenth of the respondents. The Scheduled Tribes have a very low representation in the sample with 2.4%. Gender-wise female respondents have a little edge over their male counterparts in the case of OBCs (36.8) and Scheduled Tribes (STs – 3.2%).

(4) Most of the respondents (97.2%) of the study are Hindi speaking; however, two other linguistic groups, namely, Bengali-speaking and Telegu-speaking respondents have very little representation with 2.4% and 0.4% respectively. When the data are analyzed on gender line almost a similar trend is observed.

(5) The percentage of unmarried respondents is much higher (82.4%) in comparison to the married respondents (17.6%). Among the married respondents, the proportion of married women is high (65.9%) in comparison to their counterpart married men (34.1%), which is a little less than half of the female married respondents. This suggests that marriage is still an important social custom for females in comparison to males. It further leads us to read about the age limit for marriage prevailing in society.

(6) The majority of the respondents who are married belong to the age group above 25 (84.1%) followed by the age group of 20–25 (13.6%). The age group below 20 has a little representation (2.3%) showing that in the modern Indian Social system, the age of 25 is considered as a standard age for marriage customaries.

(7) Less than one fifth (6.8%) are in secondary education, almost one fifth (19.2%) among them are intermediate passed and 7.2% have posed technical education showing a good percentage in a medium level of education, i.e. 33.2%, a few more than one fifth (22.8%) among them are

graduate and showing a high level of education. A few more than two fifth (40.8%) among them are postgraduates creating the majority group in the category of a very high level of education. Only a few (3.2%) among them are professionally skilled constituting less than one-fifth of the youths collectively showing a very low number in the very high educational category. Overall, the majority is in a very high level of education, i.e., 44.0%. The data indicate that the educational awareness among the youths is high. If we look at the sex-wise then also it can be found that in the case of female, the majority covers postgraduate (35.2%) and graduates (25.6%) followed by intermediates (22.4%). The concentration in technical (9.6%) and professional sections (3.2%) are comparatively low. The data clearly show the fact that the educational distribution among both genders is almost equal. Most of the population in the region are aware of the educational importance though there is a need to increase the conditions and facilities for technical and professional education in the near future.

(8) The majority of the age group below 20 years is found in the secondary level of education (6.8%), followed by intermediate (4.8%) and technical (1.2%) making the entire 12.8% of the population in this category, the all other sections comprise more in the age group of 20–25 especially the postgraduate section, i.e. 87.3% and professional section, i.e. 62.5%. It indicates the fact that those who are above the age group of 25 are primarily either postgraduates or professionally trained. Whereas the age group of 20–25 can be termed as the age group of people who are mainly graduates or pursuing technical training. And below 20 are mainly in the age groups for secondary or intermediate education.

(9) A little less than one-fifth of the youths (17.6%) are married while more than four-fifths among them (82.4%) are unmarried. Among the 44 respondents who are married, the spouse of most of them are highly educated (graduates 52.3%), while one-fourth (25%) of the spouses are postgraduate and a few (6.8%) spouses have professional qualifications. Only 15.9% of the spouses are educated up to intermediate level. In the case of male respondents ($N = 15$), 46.7% of spouses are graduate (High level) against 55.2% of their female counterparts. Similarly, husband spouses have an edge over their counterpart (wife) in the case of post-graduation with 31% and 13.3% respectively. At the intermediate level, there are no significant differences among the spouses on the gender line.

Globalized Technologies and Modernity: An Assessment   71

(10) Among the respondents 61.4% have come from rural backgrounds while a little less than two-fourth (38.6%) of them come from an urban background. Those spouses who have intermediate levels of education belong to rural background respondents. Among the graduate spouses, about four-fifths (78.3%) belong to rural background respondents while only 11.7% of spouses belong to urban background respondents. Among the postgraduate and professionally educated spouses the proportion of urban background respondents is high.

(11) In the case of a father's education the majority (30.8%) consists of the high level of education, i.e., at the graduation level. The second highest population of the study belongs to the intermediate section (24.4%), which comes under the category of medium level of education. The population studied in technical education (12.0%), which is also a medium level of education consists of quite a good number. This is followed by postgraduates (15.2%) make up about one-sixth population with a very high level of education. Apart from the educational level of respondents' fathers in secondary (8.4%) and primary (2.4%) are considerably low. Only a few (6.8%) of them are professionally trained. One of the striking features is that in all the categories the people either belonged to General Castes or Other Backward categories showing that these two social categories are much exposed to education.

(12) In the case of the father's education the role of geographical dimensions is not a very effective factor. As responded, the percentage is in very high level of education. Most of the respondents (71.2%) are from rural backgrounds and a little more than one-fourth of respondents have an urban background. In the case of medium and high levels of education also the percentage of rural natives is quite high with 73.2% and 87.0% respectively. Thus, the representation of rural background respondents is high at all levels of the father's education.

(13) The level of mother's education is perpetuated more at the medium level of education with 65.6%, followed by high and very high levels of education with 19.6% and 10.4% respectively. At the low level, i.e., primary level, only 4.4% of mothers are found in the study sample.

(14) In the case of mother's education, one of the most striking features is that among general caste category respondents, the level of mother's education is highest (61.4%) at a medium level of education followed by a high level of education with about one-fifth (21.6%) of respondent's mothers. While at the very high-level category only a little more than

one-tenth (12.1%) of respondent's mothers are found. Among the OBC category respondents, the mother's education level is highest (70.7%) at a medium level of education followed by a high level of education and a very high level of education with 15.9% and 12.2%, respectively. Among the SC category respondents, the mother's level of education is confined to the high level of education (23.3%) but it is highly perpetuated at a medium level of education with 70.0%. In the case of ST respondents, the mother's education level goes further low and reaches up to the medium level of education (66.7% at the medium level and 33.3% at the primary level). This suggests that caste has a significant bearing on a mother's level of education.

(15) Among the rural background respondents, the level of the mother's education was very high with 90.1% at the medium level of education, followed by those respondents whose mothers had low levels of education (6.0%). Only very few (3.9%) respondents have a graduate mother. Among the urban background respondents, the level of the mother's education is high at the graduation level. It is followed by those whose mother's education level is very high (38.2%). No urban background respondents have a primary educated mother. It suggests a significant relationship between the rural-urban background of the respondent and the level of the mother's education.

(16) A little more than half (52.4 %) of the respondents are students or unemployed youth. The remaining (47.6%) respondents are engaged in some occupational activity. About one-tenth of the respondents are engaged in government service (11.6%) and white-collar jobs (11.2%). Only a few (6.0%) of the respondents are professionals. Semi-professionals also have a low representation with 4.8%. Some of the respondents are also engaged in the occupations like small business (4.8%) and skilled workers. No respondents are engaged as unskilled workers or agriculturists. Thus, most of the youth except students/unemployed youth are in upper-middle and middle-class occupations with few exceptions.

(17) Sex-wise distribution of the respondents indicates that the percentage of females is relatively high among the students/unemployed respondents at 56.5% in comparison to the male respondents with 43.5%. Among the govt. officers/executives/managers male respondents (58.6%) have an edge over their counterpart female respondents (41.4%). Among the professionals, male respondents (75.0%) have dominated over female

Globalized Technologies and Modernity: An Assessment

respondents (25.0%). A similar pattern can be seen in the case of semi-professional jobs where male respondents (58.3%) have an edge over female respondents (41.7%). Among the white-collar jobs, female respondents have a relatively high percentage with 60.7% against their male counterparts (39.3%). Among petty business and skilled workers number of male respondents is more than female respondents.

(18) Among the student/unemployed respondents most of the respondents (92.4%) have a rural background. The representation of urban youth in this category is very low with 7.6%. Among the govt. officers/managers/ executives of urban background respondents have an edge with 55.1% over rural background youth (44.8%). Among the professionals, urban background respondents (58.35) have a relatively high representation in comparison to rural background youth (41.7%). Similar trends are observed in the case of semi-professions and white-collar occupations as well. While among the petty business and skilled workers, the predominance of rural youth can be seen.

(19) Among the male respondents, 88% are unmarried. Among the remaining married male respondents, 80% of spouses are housewives. Only one-fifth of them have a working wife engaged in white-collar jobs. However, in the case of female respondents, 76.8% are unmarried and only 23.2% of female respondents are married. Among their spouses (husbands), more than one-third (34.5%) are unemployed. As many as 44.8% of them are in white-collar jobs followed by professionals (10.3%), govt. officers/executives/managers (6.9%) and petty business (3.44%).

(20) The data show that among the rural background respondents, the majority (85.2%) of them are unmarried, and only 14.8% of respondents are married. Among these married rural background respondents, as many as 51.9% have a housewife/unemployed husband. The majority of them (44.4%) are in white-collar occupations followed by those who are in petty business (3.7%). While among the urban background respondents, three-fourths (75%) are unmarried, and only one-fourth are married. Among these married urban background respondents, the spouses of a little less than half (47.1%) are either housewives or unemployed. A significant number of spouses (29.4%) are in white-collar jobs followed by those who are engaged in professional (17.7%) and govt. officers/executives/managers (11.8%).

74   Globalization and the Transitional Cultures

(21) The father of more than one-fourth (27.6%) of the respondents were in white-collar jobs closely followed by those who were in govt. officers/executives/managers (23.2%). A significant proportion of respondents' fathers were in petty business (13.6%). One-tenth (10%) of each of the respondent's fathers were in semi-professions and unskilled jobs. A little less than one-tenth (9.6%) of respondents' fathers were agriculturists. Very few respondents' fathers were engaged as professionals (2.0%) and skilled workers (4.0%).

(22) Among the General castes respondent's father's occupations are concentrated in two occupational categories, namely Govt. officers/executives/managers and White Collar Occupations with 26.5% and 25.0% respectively. Petty business (12.9%), unskilled workers (11.5%), and semi-professions are other significant occupational categories in which respondents' fathers are engaged. Agriculture has also been found to be a significant occupational category (8.3%) in the case of respondents' fathers. Skilled workers and professionals have very low representation in the case of respondents' fathers with 3.8% and 3.0% respectively.

(23) Among the OBC respondents' white-collar occupations have the highest representation for their father with 31.7%. It is followed by govt. officers/executives and managers (19.5%), petty business (14.6%), and agriculturists (12.2%). Other occupational categories, namely, semi-professions (10.9%), skilled workers (6.0%), and unskilled workers have low representation in respondents' fathers' generation.

(24) Among the SC respondents' fathers, white collars have high representation with 23.3%, followed by govt. officers/executives/managers petty businessmen and unskilled workers (16.7% each). Semi-professions and agriculturalists have low representation with 13.3% and 10%, respectively. Professionals (3.3%) have the lowest representation among the fathers of SC respondents.

(25) Among the ST respondents, the father's occupation was confined to only three occupational categories, namely, white-collar occupations (50%), govt. officers/executives/managers (33.3%), and unskilled workers (16.7%). Thus, white-collar occupations and govt. officers/executives/managers are two occupations having representation from all caste categories due to the reservation policy of the state in the respondents' fathers' generation.

Globalized Technologies and Modernity: An Assessment

(26) Among the rural background respondent's fathers were engaged more in unskilled and skilled works and agricultural activities in contrast to their urban counterparts. Although they also have representation on the upper side of the occupational ladder, it was relatively low in comparison to their urban counterparts.

(27) Among the respondents' mothers, as many as 71.2% of them are housewives. Only 28.8% of them are working. Out of these working mothers, most (37.5%) of them are in white-collar jobs followed by agriculturists (23.6%) and skilled workers (20.8%). Only about one-tenth (9.7%) of them are officers/executives/managerial positions. A few of them (8.3%) are also engaged in petty business activities.

(28) The data show that among the General caste's respondents, the mother's occupation is highest among the white-collar jobs (9.8%) followed by skilled jobs (8.3%), petty business (4.5%), and agriculture (3.8%). Other occupations either have low representation or no representation at all.

(29) Among the OBC respondents white-collar jobs also counted for 15.9% followed by agriculture (7.3%) and govt. officers/executives/managers job (6.1%). Other occupations either have low representation or no representation at all.

(30) Among the SC respondents, the mother's occupation was confined to agriculture (20%) only while among the ST respondents. It was limited to white-collar jobs (16.7%) and skilled work (33.3%).

(31) The proportion of housewife mothers among different caste categories also varies. It was highest among the SC respondents with 89% followed by General Castes' respondents (72.0%), OBC (68.3%), and STs (50.0%).

(32) The majority of the housewife mothers belong to rural background respondents, i.e. (88.2%) in comparison to urban background respondents. In the case of rural background respondents, mothers were confined to three occupational categories, namely, agriculture (9.3%), petty business (3.3%), and white-collar jobs (1.1%). It suggests their limited mobility on the occupational ladder. In the case of urban respondents, a sharp difference can be observed as 69.1% of them are working mothers.

(33) In the case of more than one-third (36.8%) of respondents, the mother is engaged in a white-collar job. About one-tenth (10.3%) of them have the prestigious job of govt. officer/executive/manager. A little more than two-fifths (22.1%) of urban respondents' mothers are engaged in skilled occupations. Thus, in the mother's generation of the respondents, we see a sharp difference in their occupational status.

(34) More than half of the respondents (55.2%) reside in rented houses in the region and are actually from rural areas while even less than one-fifth of the population, i.e., 17.6% though belonging to rural places still have their own house in the region. A little more than one-fourth of the population (27.2%) are such who belong to an urban background originally and also have their residence in the region itself. Thus, 44.8% of respondents overall have their own house in the Allahabad region.

(35) Most of the respondents (66.4%) possess agricultural land, more than three-fourth percentage of the studied population have their own house at their native place, and a little less than half (46.0%) of the respondents have plots though the majority (54.0%) don't possess any plot. More than half of the studied population (55.2%) lives in rented houses, while the remaining 44.8% have their own house in their current locality. Besides none of the respondents have any kind of factory or company.

(36) More than half or two-fourths of the respondents (55.6%) have an average level of consumption of material goods like electronics, home, and computer appliances, cars, etc. in the region creating a majority in this section. It is followed by a high level of consumption (31.2%) among more than one-fourth of respondents. It shows that the youth in the region are moving speedily from an average level to a high level of consumption. It also reveals the fact that the region is moving toward economic growth and has seen an increase in per-capita income in recent times. Further, very few respondents (2.4%) also belong to a very high level of consumption category. The remaining respondents belong to the category of low level of consumption (10.0%) and very low level of consumption (0.8%) but they are just one-fourth of the total clubbing together. While the distribution is seen gender-wise then a notable fact here is that the number of females with high and very high levels of consumption (17.2% & 2.0% respectively) is more than the number of males (14.0% & 0.4% respectively) points out to the fact that the level of consumption of goods among females are higher than the males.

(37) The percentage of high and very high levels of consumption is higher in the natives of urban areas, i.e. (74.4%) and (100.0%) respectively, in comparison to rural areas, whereas the percentage of very low and low consumption patterns is higher (100.0%) among the natives of rural areas. But the higher percentage of the average level of consumption among the natives of rural areas (97.1%), which is also highest in numbers in overall consumption pattern (55.6%) shows that the rural areas are also heading toward higher living standards rapidly in the upcoming days in respect of consumption pattern.

ASSESSING THE EXPOSURE TO COMMUNICATION TECHNOLOGIES

Globalization is very closely related to the process of communication. In modern society, the level of mass media exposure is relatively high, which has an important bearing on the worldview of a person, and it is directly related to the process of modernity. Globalization has had a deep impact on mass media in the last three decades. As a result, modern mass media communication has been transformed into a Global Communication System. Globalization of mass media is an important process in a society like India. In pre-globalization era, the Indian communication system was bifurcative consisting of the urban communicative system, which was largely based on modern mass media, and the rural communication system which relied more on traditional modes of communication, i.e. face-to-face and oral communication.

Modern mass media communication could not penetrate the rural Hinterlands, as it requires some level of literacy to use print media and the capacity to afford audio-visual, media, like television. Therefore, except for radio, most of the mass media are confined to urban areas.

In the decades of 1990s, television penetrated most of the rural areas of India. This process has been further strengthened by the penetration of mobile telephony in rural areas in the last two decades. Thus, today television and mobile phones (both feature phones and smartphones) made it possible to link the rural masses to the global communication system.

In the present study, it is observed that 95% of the respondents subscribe to a newspaper. The vernacular (Hindi) print media is the most popular among the respondents. On average, 7 out of 10 respondents prefer to read Hindi newspapers. Most of the newspapers have adopted digital technology for printing and with the use of computers and Internet-based technology have integrated the local and the global on one platform. Most of the Hindi newspapers publish the front page with local news most of the time, but on a certain occasion, they prefer national and international news headlines depending upon the news. Thus, Hindi newspapers to a great extent are local editions. English newspapers have local, regional, national, and international contents. This kind of transformation of newspapers is a result of revolution in communication technologies.

Thus, a newspaper not only fulfills the local needs of the reader but also furnishes information on regional, national, and transnational events and issues. Among the broadcast media radio which was a very popular medium both in urban and rural areas of India has lost its credentials in the era of globalization, although the emergence and popularity of FM radio has helped in the incarnation of the radio both at the local and national level. Some FM channels are broadcast at the National level, but several FM channels broadcast their programs only at the local level.

Internet radio has made a global reach of the local radio channels. Respondents for the present. The study says largely (87.2%) use their mobile phone to listen to FM radio. This indicates that the respondents use radio to fulfill their entertainment needs and various kinds of local and global information provided by these entertainment channels of FM radio. However, the traditional radio sets based on analog technologies have been quite unpopular among the respondents.

Cinema, which has been a major form of mass media for providing entertainment to the masses, has been badly affected in the era of globalization, although the Indian film industry attempted to survive by transforming the infrastructure of cinema going from traditional types of cinema halls to the multiplex and PVRs, which became an important element of malls in urban areas. But the rise of Internet-based communication technologies and the shifting of the masses to these new communication, technologies put a new challenge to the cinema industry. Not only television but also computers and mobile phones became alternative forms of cinema halls. The youths of the present study used to go to the cinema, but the frequency of cinema-going varies among them. But the majority of them (40.8%) used to go to the cinema quarterly. Very few of them go to the cinema monthly (6.4%) or once in two months (16.8%). The rest of them used to go to the cinema half-yearly or annually. This trend among the youth suggests that they go to the cinema only occasionally. Their entertainment needs are fulfilled by other mediums.

Within the DVD player, it has lost its popularity among the youth as only a few, 6.8% of the respondents watch films on DVD players. Most of the respondents, i.e. 98%, watch films at their homes. Hindi films are watched by most of the respondents (78.8%). Cent percent of respondents have a DTH/cable connection in their home, but they watch TV occasionally (57.6%). It suggests that the youth are less dependent on television to fulfill their media needs.

It suggests that the dependency of the youth on New Media, particularly on mobile phones, has improved technology tremendously. Frequency of using the Internet is very high (90.8%). Most of the youth of the present study spent more than 2 hours on the Internet daily for different purposes like video conferencing, e-commerce, entertainment, etc. Most of the youth 95.2% affirm that the Internet helps establish new relationships (virtual relationships). Most of them use email and blogs social. Social networking sites like Facebook and WhatsApp are highly popular among the respondents, which shows that most of the youth have a varied means of mass media exposure from newspapers, to Facebook to WhatsApp and analysis of their mass media exposure indicates that 7 out of every 10 have an average mass media exposure and about 3 of every 10 have high media exposure. Very few of the respondents have (0.8%) low media exposure. It seems that average mass media exposure of the youth has some relationship with the social background like respondents' native place, the occupation of the respondents, the occupation of father and mother, the native place of the parents, their household consumption pattern, etc.

As far as the dynamics of material culture are concerned, all the respondents use e-commerce sites but the frequency of using these sites is low among the respondents. The tendency of purchasing stuff online is also low among the respondents, which is highest for clothes 33.2%, followed by home and kitchen needs 24.8%, books 20.8%, and electronics 18%. This suggests that most of the youths purchase the stuff online. Online order of food is preferred by most of the respondents (80.4%). The majority of the youth (63.6%) prefer to buy branded clothes from clothing malls (20.4%), Reliance Trends (16.8%), and other brands like Levi's, etc. (13.6%). More than one-third of the youth still depend on local markets to buy clothes. About four out of five youths watch online channels like Netflix (35.6%), Jio TV (17.6%), and Amazon Prime (12.4%).

Most of the youths see the interaction between boys and girls over mobile phones with a positive attitude. About one-third of the respondents are quite traditional in their views on the issue of intercaste marriage. However, others are more open to intercaste and love marriage but reluctant to interreligious marriages. Half of the respondents are not in favor of marriage through Internet matrimonial. The majority of the respondents feel that internet has changed the attitude toward working women at least to some extent.

The above findings of this study indicate that there is a significant shift in the youth, not only in the use of branded stuff in their daily life but it also has a positive impact on their attitude toward working women and issues related to matrimony and marriages. Thus, the process of globalization along with mass media exposure has an important impact on the material culture and the attitude of the respondents. analysis of levels of modernity through various items on the O.M. scale indicates that the level of modernity is concentrated from average to high levels of modernity, as almost 56.0% of the respondents have an average level of modernity, and a significant number of the respondents have a high level of modernity (43.6%). No respondents have a low level of modernity in the case of material culture.

It suggests that the level of modernity has some relationship with the social background and the levels of mass media exposure. The relationship between the levels of mass media exposure and levels of modernity indicates that among those who have average mass media exposure, more than half (55.4%) had a medium level of modernity. A significant proportion of them (44.0%) have a high level of modernity. It means that there is a positive relationship between the levels of mass media exposure and levels of modernity, but it does not solely depend on mass media exposure. There may be some other factors affecting modernity. The respondents having a high level of mass media exposure also have a medium level of modernity (56. 2 %) in terms of non-material culture.

This strengthens our above observation regarding the complicated relationship between the levels of mass media exposure and the levels of modernity. Therefore, we have to examine the relationship between nonmaterial variables related to social structure concerning the levels of modernity.

THE CASE OF NONMATERIAL CULTURE

To understand the levels of modernity in the O.M. scale under nonmaterial culture, various variables like thoughts on free interaction between boys and girls over mobile phones, types of marriages preferred most, opinions on marriages through Internet matrimonial, the impact of the internet on attitude toward working women, impact of mass media on local cultures, desirability of practicing family planning, continuity of purdah system (veiling system) in the family, level preferred for education to daughter, job preferred for daughter, views on qualification for holding a high office and most important thing for the progress of the country, etc. were taken into consideration.

The data reveal that the majority, i.e., more than half (56.0%) of the respondents have an average level of modernity in terms of nonmaterial culture followed by almost two-fourths of other respondents (43.6%) who are at a higher level of modernity. 4% of the respondents have a very high level of modernity while no respondents were found in the low or very low levels of modernity. The data indicates that though the majority is highest in the average section, but the country is moving rapidly toward a high level of modernity and soon it can be expected that the number in the very high level of modernity will also increase as there is already inclusion in that category too which is a very good sign for the development of the country in terms of nonmaterial aspects. Sex-wise though more female respondents (57.1%) can be found in the average level of modernity but the number in the higher level of modernity is dominated by male respondents (58.7%). But the notable fact here is that the difference between the two genders in the higher level of modernity is very marginal which shows females have very impressive numbers in levels of modernity which shortly may rise at a good level. The country is going through a transition phase. It is continuously moving from an average level to a high level of modernity. Due to this transition, some subsequent changes have also been noticed in the cultural processes, for example, in the shopping culture, the food culture, the Clothing culture, or the entertainment culture of the youths where the modernity rate is high to very high but in non-material culture, the impact of globalization is still in transition.

Apart from this, the analysis of the relationship between caste and level of modernity reveals that there is a variation among the caste at the medium and high levels of modernity. Among the general caste, the medium level of modernity is relatively high 56.8%. In the case of OBCs, it has gone up to 58.5%. As far as the case of SC and ST respondents is concerned, 53.3% of the respondents have a high level of modernity. Among the ST level of modernity is high with 50%. It suggests that General and OBC caste respondents are relatively more conservative than the SC and ST respondents. The relationship between this level of Education of the respondents and their modernity level shows that those who have a medium level of education, a little more than half of them, have a medium level of modernity and almost half of them have a high level of modernity. Almost a similar pattern is observed with high levels of education.

Six out of every ten have a medium level of modernity, and only four of every 10 have a high level of modernity. It suggests that although modern education is considered the vehicle of modernity, in the case of the present study modernity is perpetuated at a medium level. Only half of the respondents have reached a too-high level of modernity in the case of a high level of education as well as with a medium level of education. Thus, education has a positive relationship with modernity, but not in absolute terms. There are other factors like caste to religion, which may limit the level of modernity in a particular social category. Linguistic groups also seem to be an important variable in the case of the level of modernity. The study finds that Hindi-speaking respondents are more stagnant at the medium level of modernity in comparison to Bengali- and Telegu-speaking respondents among whom the high level of modernity raised to 66.7% and 65.2% respectively. It is clear from both facts that there are regional variations among the respondents based on their linguistic identity, social background, and mass media exposure together operating in a complicated manner in determining the level of modernity in the present study.

The above-mentioned findings of the study throw light on the intricate relationship between globalization, communication, and cultural change. This study is focused on the youth. Most of the youth are highly educated having educated parents. They are largely unmarried and about half of them are students and unemployed youths.

SUMMARY

The majority of the country is still from rural backgrounds and average levels of consumption patterns of material goods. These characteristics of the sample reflect the sociocultural milieu of the respondents, as most of the respondents or their parents are first-migrant generations from rural areas. It may have an important bearing not only on their patterns of mass media communication but also on their material and nonmaterial culture. Culture, as a result of globalized technologies of mass media communication, has been revolutionized in the last three decades. Globalization has integrated all forms of modern mass media communication and brought them on the platform on one platform, that is a mobile phone. The spread of mobile phones empowered with push message technology and the Internet has enhanced the process of economic, political, and cultural globalization.

These communication Technologies are at the heart of globalization (Singh, 2004, 2007). The modernity generated by globalization is reflexive in the sense that it is not possible to separate cause-and-effect relationships between different variables. So, on one hand, communication technology plays an important role in the process of economic globalization by supporting digital transactions and communication at the global level, on the other hand, the equipment and gadgets of communication are produced.

Distributed global software and hardware industries are transforming the mode and technology of communication, which generates a new impetus for globalization. Thus, the complicated relationship between globalization and communication is analyzed in the present study at two levels: (i) at the level of modern mass media communication, which includes print media (based on printing technology, which helps in the development of modernity in modern Europe since 15th century) and (ii) broadcasting media, mainly radio and audiovisual media like television, which is based on radiowave technology of communication that is analog.

New communication technologies are mainly based on digital technologies. One major difference between modern mass media based on analog technology and new media based on digital technology is that modern mass media are capable of transmitting the message, image, and sound at a distant place simultaneously, but lag in getting the feedback. In one sense, it was one-way communication. There was no provision of knowing the reaction of the receiver of the message. But the new media is based on interactive technology of communication and provides a digital platform to its users. They send and receive messages instantaneously at the global level.

This interactive capacity of new media has wide implications not only in integrating the existing modern mass media into a global communication system but also in empowering the users to have a varied experience of mass media communication.

Globalization has a wider process that provides material conditions for cultural change. Globalization is not merely globalization is not merely a structural process of change. The dynamics of cultural change can be analyzed at two levels: (i) in terms of non-material culture and (ii) in terms of material culture. The process of globalization has a great impact on the lifestyle of the youth, in terms of their eating habits, dressing patterns, and use of branded consumer products, which reflects the transformation in the material culture. At the same time, globalization has an important bearing on the nonmaterial culture, that is norms, beliefs, and values on the youths are more exposed to globalized media and adopting norms, values, and beliefs of "high modernity".

Therefore, the present chapter is focused on the patterns of material culture among the youth as well as on understanding the worldview of the respondents in terms of their levels of modernity. Giddens used the term high modernity/late modernity. Bauman used the term solid modernity/liquid modernity. Beck talks of reflexive modernity. Habermas talks about "modernity is an unfinished project." All these thinkers as asserted that the phenomenon of modernity is not over, but globalization has strengthened modernity and modernity is transforming itself into a new form, which has been identified as high modernity/late modernity/liquid modernity/reflexive modernity.

Thus, globalization in the present study is analyzed in terms of the levels of modernity of the respondents. Some scholars of postmodernism and globalization have analyzed these processes in terms of consumer culture, and they say that contemporary society is a consumer society. Therefore, we have analyzed not only patterns of consumer culture among the respondents in terms of their material aspects but also their levels of modernity. The results in this regard are very clear that the globalization factor has done a revolutionary change in terms of communication technologies. The mass media exposure and level of consumption of materialistic lifestyle varies from high to very high level but as soon as we move toward the nonmaterialistic culture, the level of modernity drops down toward a shift from average to high level. Hence, the chapter indicates the fact that developing countries like India are deeply rooted in its culture and hence if the question of the high level of modernity arises then it is not possible to uproot the country from its years-old ancient customs. Rather the solution is to change the global elements to its local culture and strengthen the learning process in the country with a value-based holistic approach. The newly reformed New Educational Policy 2020 also known as NEP – 2020 can be a milestone in this regard that has given a special focus on Indian Knowledge Systems to create a holistic development through its neighborhood skills and its effect on the culture and modernity must be studied in the future. Thus, the chapter opens a new scope of study for the researchers of future generations to examine the educational system and level of modernity, especially in the case of middle-class youth, which is also the backbone of the present society to enhance the culture in the upcoming years and make India truly a *Vishwaguru* (the global teacher).

7

EPILOGUE: PUTTING THE THREADS TOGETHER

Based on the major findings of this study and the above discussions, some conclusions can be drawn as follows:

(1) Globalization is a wider process of social transformation, affecting all the societies of the world. However, its impact is different in all the societies conditioned by the local socialcultural milieu, which may promote or check the process of sociocultural transformation in a given society. In developing societies like India, caste, language, religion, and rural-urban background are important factors that can check the rise of modernity at a certain level. In the context of the present study, level of modernity in the case of nonmaterial culture is perpetuated at a medium level of modernity. Even highly educated youth have stagnated at a medium level of modernity. Though it is moving toward a high level, the process is slow and hence there is a need to increase the process of *glocalization of education* in this case rather than adoption of Westernized ideologies to create a society that is more developed also in terms of its cultural values.

(2) The communication theorists, like Schramm and Daniel Learner emphasized that communication technologies can modernize a society and can change the worldview of the recipient of the message. Learner particularly says that if a society with a 30% literacy rate is exposed to mass media, it helps in the process of modernization of the given society. Thus, the combination of education and mass media exposure plays an important role in the modernization of developing societies. According to the report of Forbes.com, only in Facebook, India has the largest number of users with 448.1 million users, which is 31.8% of the country's population.

This percentage itself is higher than the estimated media literacy rate given by Daniel Learner for the globalization of media helping in the modernization process. The overall social media exposure is 33.4% with 398.0 million users. But in most cases, these social media platforms serve as entertainment platforms rather than knowledge-producing platforms creating a less effective correlation between communication and globalization in terms of nonmaterial culture in Eastern societies like India.

These theories of the above-mentioned communication theories are also found partially correct by Singh (2002). He found that the level of education and level of mass media exposure have some positive relationship with the level of modernity, but not in absolute terms. It is a complicated process in which several factors impinge upon the process of modernity in a traditional society like India. Only under certain conditions, level of high modernity can be achieved. In the case of the present study also it has been established that communication theorists view that the level of education and modernity are sufficient conditions to transform a traditional society into a modern society is not enough for the countries having Eastern ideologies as they are more rooted to their traditional values and belief systems.

(3) The authors of globalization theories also expressed similar type of views and typified globalization as a process of high modernity. India has now experienced three decades of globalization along with a communication revolution. According to the globalization theory of Anthony Giddens, the modernity level of those have been exposed to globalization and new communication technologies could have achieved a high level of modernity, but in a region like India which has been a region of holy pilgrimage center for centuries, the exposure to higher education and higher level of media exposure are not successful in achieving the high level of modernity. The process of traditional society order perhaps checked the process of modernity and perpetuated it at the medium level.

Hence, we can conclude that globalization and new communication technology are important factors in the homogenization of culture. But in the case of a developing society like India, the level of modernity depends upon factors like caste, language, religion, and the rural-urban background of a person. To raise the level of modernity, one needs to develop all these checkpoints of the existing society layer by layer. While the problems of caste, language, religion, gender stereotypes, etc. can be solved by an education system that is inclusive other factors like rural–urban divisions can be solved through economic progression. Globalization highly impacts the material cultures of these societies like food culture, cloth culture, and other popular cultures but when it comes to nonmaterial culture, the outreach of globalization becomes limited in those societies which are highly value-based. Thus, there is a need to reformulate the thesis put forward by Giddens (1996) that "globalization is a higher stage of modernity" in the case of the Eastern perspective.

BIBLIOGRAPHY

Allen, A. (2021). Feminist perspectives on power. In E. N. Zalta, & U. Nodelman (Eds.), *The stanford encyclopedia of philosophy* (Fall 2022 Edition). https://plato.stanford.edu/archives/fall2022/entries/feminist-power/

Appadurai, A. (1996). *Modernity at large: Cultural dimensions of globalization.* University of Minnesota Press.

Arendt, H. (1958). *The human condition.* The University of Chicago Press.

Armstrong, E. (2020). *Marxist and socialist feminism.* Study of Women and Gender: Faculty Publications. https://scholarworks.smith.edu/swg_facpubs/15

B., Axford (Ed.) (2021). *Why globalization matters: Engaging with theory in rethinking globalizations.* Routledge. GBR ISBN 978-1-03-205630-2.

Bauman, Z. (1999). *Culture as Praxis.* Sage Publications.

Bean, A. M. (2016). Venezuela, human rights and participatory democracy. *Critical Sociology, 42*(6), 827–843.

Bell, D. (1960). *The end of ideology.* Free Press.

Berlo, D. K. (2020, October 12). The Process of Communication. Free download, borrow, and streaming. *Internet Archive.* https://archive.org/details/dli.ernet.235577

Bodhi, S. R., & Jojo, B. (2019). *The problematics of tribal integration: Voices from India's Alternative Center.* The Shared Mirror Publishing House.

Brown. (1999). Globalization and cultural conflict in developing countries: The South African Example on JSTOR. www.jstor.org. https://www.jstor.org/stable/20644725

Burns, R. W. (2004). *Communications: An international history of the formative years.* The Institution of Engineering and Technology. 978-0-86341-327-8.

Castells, M. (1991). *The Informational City: A New Framework for Social Change.* Centre for Urban and Community Studies, University of Toronto.

Castells, M. (1996). *The Rise of Network Society.* Wiley-Blackwell Publishers.

Census. (2011). *Government of India*. http://censusindia.gov.in

Cruz-Saco, M. A. (2018). Indigenous communities and social inclusion in Latin America. Paper presented at *Expert Group Meeting on Family Policies for Inclusive Societies*, New York Headquarters, United States, 1–22. https://www.un.org/development/desa/family/wp-content/uploads/sites/23/2018/05/2-1.pdf

Cvetkovich, A., & Kellner, D. (1997). *Articulating the global and the local: Globalization and cultural studies*. Westview Press.

Dicken, P. (2007). *Global shift: Mapping the changing contours of the world economy*. SAGE.

Dimitrova, A. (2002). Challenging globalization-the contemporary sociological debate about globalization a theoretical approach. *M.A Dissertation in Advanced European and International Studies. Center International de formation Europeenee* (p. 70).

Doshi, J. K. (1984). Communication and national integration: A study of Hindu Muslim relationship. *Communicator*, 24–31.

Dubois, C. (1955). *Ralph Linton. The tree of culture*. Alfred A. Knopf. xiv, 692, xvi.

Durkheim, E. (1915). *The elementary forms of the religious life*. Allen and Unwin.

Durkheim, É. (1960). *The division of labor in society*. Free Press. 4th print.

Eggertsson, T. (2010). Mapping social technologies in the cultural commons. *U.S: Cornell law review*, 95, 711–732.

Enman, C. (1999). *One against the world*. The Ottawa Citizen.

Flew, T. (2007). *Understanding global media* (1st ed). Palgrave Macmillan.

Fernandez-Kelly, P. (2007). The global assembly line in the new millennium: A review essay. *Signs: Journal of Women in Culture and Society*, 32(2), 509–521.

Friedman, T. (1999). *The Lexus and the Olive Tree*. Farrar Straus Giroux.

Ghosh, B. (2011). Cultural changes and challenges in the era of globalization: The case of India. *Journal of Developing Societies*, 27(2), 153–175. https://doi.org/10.1177/0169796X1102700203

Ghurye. (1959). *The Scheduled Tribes*. Popular Book House.

Bibliography

Ghurye, G. S. (1963). *The Scheduled Tribes*. Popular Prakashan.

Giddens, A. (1990). *The consequences of modernity*. Stanford University Press.

Habermas, J., & Blazek, J. R. (1987). The idea of the university: Learning processes. *New German Critique*, (41), 3–22.

Hardt, M., & Negri, A. (2000). *Empire*. Harvard University Press.

Harvey, D. (1989). *The condition of postmodernity: An enquiry into the origins of cultural change*. Wiley.

Held, D., McGrew, A., Goldblatt, D., & Perraton, J. (1999). *Global transformations: Politics, economics and culture*. Polity Press.

Hirst, P. Q., & Thompson, G. F. (1996). *Globalization in question: The international economy and the possibilities of governance*. Polity Press.

Hosseini, H. M. (2010). Popular culture in Asia: Globalization, regionalization, and localization. *Procedia-Social and Behavioral Sciences*, 2, 7356–7358.

Huntington, S. (1996). *The clash of civilizations and the remaking of world order*. Simon & Schuster.

Inkeles, A., & Smith, D. M. (1974). *Becoming modern*. Harvard University Press.

Jaja, J. M. (2010). Globalization or Americanization: Implication for Sub-Saharan Africa. In the book: *Globalization - Today, Tomorrow* (1st edition).

Lee, D. (2018). *Independent television production in the UK: From cottage industry to big business*. Palgrave Macmillan.

Lerner, D. (1958). *The passing of traditional society: Modernizing the middle east*. The Free Press.

Lerner, D., & Pevsner, L. W. (1958). *The passing of traditional society: Modernizing the middle east*. Free Press.

Linton, R. (1955). *The tree of culture*. Alfred A. Knopf.

Lynd, R. S., & Lynd, H. M. (1929). *Middletown: A study in Contemporary American Culture*. Brace and Company.

MacDonald, D. (1957). A Theory of Mass Culture. In B. Rosenberg & D. W. Manning (Eds.), *Mass Culture: The Popular Arts in America* (pp. 59–73). Free Press.

Majumdar, D. N., & Madan, T. N. (1957). General and theoretical: An introduction to social anthropology, *American Anthropologist, 59*(1).

Majumdar, D. N., & Madan, T. N. (2008). *An introduction to social anthropology*. Mayoor paperbacks.

Mauss, M. (1954). *The gift forms and functions of exchange in archaic societies*. Free Press.

McClelland, D. C. (1961). *The achieving society*. Free Press.

McLuhan, M., & Powers, B. R. (1992). *The global village: Transformations in world life and media in the 21st century*. Oxford University Press.

McQuail, D. (1969). *Towards a sociology of mass communications*. Collier-Macmillan.

McQuail, D. (2006). The mediatization of war. *International Communication Gazette, 68*(2).

McQuail, D. (2010). *Mcquail's mass communication theory*. SAGE Publications.

Merriam-Webster (1828). Middle-class. *Merriam-Webster.com Dictionary*. https://www.merriam-webster.com/dictionary/middle-class

Myrdal, G. (1968). *Asian drama: An inquiry into the poverty of nations*. Pantheon.

NEP. (2020). *Policy document released by Government of India*. https://www.education.gov.in/sites/upload_files/mhrd/files/NEP_Final_English_0.pdf

Nimkoff, M. F. (1947). *A handbook of sociology (1947)*. Free download, borrow, and streaming. Internet Archive. https://archive.org/details/in.ernet.dli.2015.239785

Nisbet, R. A. (1966). *The sociological tradition*. Basic Books.

Ogburn, W. F., & Nimkoff, M. F. (1964). *A handbook of sociology*. Routledge.

Ohmae, K. (1990). *Borderless World. Power and strategy in the global marketplace*. Harper Collins.

Okin, S. M. (1989). *Justice, gender, and the family*. Basic Books.

Pieterse, N. (2004). *Globalization and culture: Global mélange*. Rowman & Littlefield Publishers.

Bibliography

Pye, L. W., & Social Science Research Council. (1963). Communications and political development. In *Conference on Communication and Political Development*. Princeton University Press.

Pye, L. W. (1963). *Communication and Political Development*. Radha Krishna Publication.

Raisa, R., & Tasnim, N. (2020). *McDonaldization of Asia: Impacts of globalization on the Asian Culture*. Available at SSRN 3702432.

Redfield, R. (1941). The folk culture of Yucatan. *KIP Monographs, 148*. https://digitalcommons.usf.edu/kip_monographs/148

Riesman, D., Glazer, N., & Denney, R. (2001). *The lonely crowd: A study of the changing American character*. Yale University Press. 978-0-300-08865-6.

Ritzer, G. (2011). *Globalization: The essentials*. Wiley.

Robertson, R. (1992). *Globalization – Social theory and global culture* (pp. 57–60). SAGE.

Rogers, E. (1962). *Diffusion of innovations*. Simon & Schuster. 978-0-7432-5823-4.

Rosengren, K. E. (1981). Mass media and social change: Some current approaches. In E. Katz & T. Szecskö (Eds.), *Mass Media and Social Change* (pp. 247–263). Sage.

Sarkar, J. (1990). *The Jarawa*. Seagull Books.

Sassen, S. (1991). *The global city*. Princeton University Press.

Scholte, J. A. (2000). *Globalization: A critical introduction*. Palgrave Macmillan.

Schramm, W., & Roberts, D. F. (1954). How communication works. In W. Schramm (Ed.). *The Process and Effects of Mass Communications*. Ill: University of Illinois Press.

Scott, J. C. (1998). *Seeing like a State: How certain schemes to improve the human condition have failed* (p. 11). Yale University Press. 978-0-30007016-3.

Sen, A. (1979). Utilitarianism and welfarism. *The Journal of Philosophy, 76*(9), 463–489.

Sharma. (2003). *Elements of Indian Civilisation: A sociological perspective on JSTOR*. www.jstor.org. https://www.jstor.org/stable/41919927

Singh, Y. (1986). *Modernization of indian tradition*. Rawat Publications.

Singh, V. P. (2004). Globalization, new communication technologies and socio- cultural change in India. *Meerut: Emerging Trends in Development Research* (p. 6). ISSN NO. 0972-9445. 11 (1&2).

Singh, V. P. (2007). Globalization and social stratification in India. *Emerging Trends in Development Research.*

Tai, E. (2003). Rethinking culture, national culture, and Japanese culture. *Japanese Language and Literature,* 37(1), 1–26.

The Baiga. (1939). *Elwin Verrier.* Free download, borrow, and streaming. Internet Archive. https://archive.org/details/dli.ernet.237649

Theiner, P. (2014). *Book Review: Theories of globalization by Barrie Axford.* https://eprints.lse.ac.uk/56156/1/blogs.lse.ac.uk-Book_Review_Theories_of_ Globalization_by_Barrie_Axford.pdf

Therborn, G. (1995). *European modernity and beyond: The trajectory of European societies 1945–2000.* SAGE Publications Ltd. https://doi.org/10. 4135/9781446222317

Therborn, G. (2001). Globalization and inequality. Issues of conceptualization and explanation. *Soziale Welt,* 52(4), 449–476. http://www.jstor.org/stable/ 40878367

Thomas, C. (2001). Global Governance, development and human security: Exploring the links. *Third World Quarterly,* 22(2), 159–175.

Tomlinson, J. (1999). *Globalization and culture.* University of Chicago Press.

Turner, B. S., & Khondker, H. H. (2010). *Globalization east and west.* SAGE Publications. 9780857026705 https://books.google.co.in/books?id=fJJxW0w mDIgC

Tylor, E. B. (1871). *Primitive culture: Researches into the development of mythology, philosophy, religion, art, and custom.* Cambridge University Press.

Ullah, A. A., & Ming Yit Ho, H. (2020). Globalisation and cultures in Southeast Asia: Demise, fragmentation, transformation. *Global Society,* 35(2), 191–206.

UN DESA. (2015). *United Nations Department of Economic and Social Affairs.* https://www.un.org/en/development/desa/news/2015.html

Virginius, X. (2005). Politics of language, religion and identity: Tribes in India. *Economic and Political Weekly,* 1363–1370.

Bibliography

Virginius Xaxa Committee Report. (2014). Report of the high level committee on socio-economic, health and educational status of tribal communities of India. *Ministry of Tribal Affairs, Government of India* (pp. 30–365).

Wallerstein, I. (2000). Globalization or the age of transition? A long-term view of the trajectory of the world-system. *International Sociology, 15*(2), 249-265. https://doi.org/10.1177/0268580900015002007

Wallerstein, I. (2004). *World-systems analysis: An introduction* (p. 21). Duke University Press.

Waltz, K. N. (1999). Globalization and governance. *Political Science and Politics, 32*(4), 693–700.

Weber, A. (1998). Civilization and culture—A synthesis "Fundamentals of culture-sociology: social process, civilizational process and culture-movement" (1921). In S. Mennell (Ed.). *Classical readings on culture and civilization* (1st ed.). Routledge. https://doi.org/10.4324/9781351227025

Xaxa, V. (1999). Tribes as indigenous people of India. *Economic and Political Weekly, XXXIV*(51), 3589–3595.

Young, I. M. (1990). *Throwing like a girl and other essays in feminist philosophy and social theory*. Indiana University Press.

INDEX

Academic thinkers, 23
Agricultural folk society, 47
Akashvani, 42–43
All India Radio (AIR), 42–43
Americanization of culture, 3
Assimilation Theory, 52
Audio-visual media, 38, 43
Ayurveda, 49–50

Berlo's model of communication,
    32–33
Bhakti movements, 13–14
Big data analytics, 44–45
Broadcast Media, 42–43
    radio, 78

Capability Approach, 11–12
Chicago School of Sociology, The,
    40
Children with Special Needs girls
    (CWSN girls), 62
Cinema, 43, 78
Civilization, 16
Clash of Civilizations, 13–14
Cloud computing, 44–45
Commercialization, 17
Communication process, 24–25,
    27, 29, 41, 48–49, 62
    assessing exposure to, 77–80
    audio-visual media, 43
    broadcast media, 42–43
    globalization and, 25–27
    models of, 31–33
    modern mass media, 42–43
    social media or new
        communication
        technologies, 44–46

theories, 86
theorists, 85–86
traditional media, 41–42
types of, 39–46
works/trends in communication
    studies, 33–39
Contemporary India, women in,
    61–62
Convergence, 13
Cosmopolitanism, 5
Creolization, 22
Cultural assimilation process,
    52
Cultural change, 24–25
Cultural convergence, 13
Cultural differentialism, 21
Cultural diffusion, 13–14
Cultural globalization, 3, 20–22,
    48–49
    and global south, 47–51
    modernity as process of,
        22–23
Cultural heterogeneities, 27
Cultural homogenization, 20–21,
    53–54
    concept, 20–21
Cultural hybridization,
    21–22
Cultural imperialism, 20
Cultural integration, 13–14
Cultural lag, 19
Cultural mediation, 36
Cultural process, 10
    globalization as, 13–14
Cultural production, 10, 20, 38
Cultural reception, 48–49

Cultural transmission, 10, 20, 48–49
Culture, 15–16, 51–52
  communication and cultural change, 24–25
  evolution and types of, 17–19
  globalization and communication, 25–27
  globalization in transforming processes of, 20–22
  modernity as process of cultural globalization, 22–23
Culture for Commons, 33

Deterritorialization concept, 6, 9
Development Communications, 31
Diffusion, 13
Diffusion of Innovation theory, 24
Digital divide, 39
Digital media, 26
Digitalization, 57
Discontinuities of Modernity, 8
Doordarshan, 43
DVD player, 78–79

Early communication research, trends of, 33–35
Eastern ideologies, 86
Economic globalization, 48
Economic process, 11–12
Education, 62, 81–82, 86–87
Empathy, 25–27
"Empire" thesis, The, 10
Equalization process, 62–63
Ethnoscapes, 15–16
Euro-centric dimension, 22–23, 50–51
Expansionalism, 20–21
Exposure to communication technologies, 77–80

Face to face communication, 31, 39–40
Facebook, 79, 85–86
Female-oriented movements, 57
Feminism concept, 58

Field of experience, 29–30
Financescape, 15–16
Financial independence, 62
Financial institutions, 12
Folk culture to urbanization, 17–19
Folk media, 30–31
Folk/tribal society, 18

General Agreement on Tariffs and Trade (GATT), 11
Geographical Indication Tag (GI Tag), 21
"Global commodity chain" concept, 12
Global communication system, 77
Global cultural flow, 15–16
Global culture, 18–19
"Global governance" concept, 12
Global south, cultural globalization and, 47–51
Globalization, 1–6, 8, 22, 34–35, 47–48, 50, 53–54, 77, 85–87
  approaches of, 8–10
  of audio-visual and broadcast media, 38
  and communication, 25–27
  as cultural process, 13–14
  of culture, 13
  process, 10, 14, 47, 80
  as process-agency approach, 9–10
  schools of, 5–8
  as structural process, 10–13
  as system-structure approach, 9
  as territory-scale approach, 9
  theories, 86
  as time–space approach, 8–9
  in transforming processes of culture, 20–22
Globalized media, 63
Glocalization of education, 21, 85
Governmental schemes, 62

Hare Krishna movement, 7–8
Hierarchical system, 22

Index

Hindi newspapers, 77–78
Hinduism, 52
Homogenization of culture, 3
Human society, 17
Hyperglobalization, 5
Hyperglobalizers, 5–6, 22–23

"Identity articulation" concept, 52
Ideoscapes, 15–16
Independent television production
    sector, 38
Indian communication system, 77
Indian society, 57–58, 64
Indian Vedic culture, 64
Indian women through ages, 59–61
Indigenous philosophical principle,
    52–53
Indus Valley civilization, The,
    59–60
Industrialization, 3, 17, 34–35
Information and Communication
    Technology (ICT), 44
Integration, 13
Integration Model, 52
Interactive technologies, 1
International Monetary Fund
    (IMF), 11
Internationalism, 5
Internationalization, 7
Internet, 27, 39
    internet-based technology,
      77–78
    matrimonial, 80
    radio, 78
Isolation theory, 52

Kasturba Gandhi Balika
    Vidyalayas (KGBVs), 62

Language, 51–52
Lesbian, Gay, Bisexual,
    Transgender, and Queer or
    Questioning community
    (*LGBTQ* community), 49
Liberal feminism, 58
Liberal feminist, 58

Linguistic groups, 81–82
Liquid modernity, 23

"Make in India" program, 21
Male respondents, 73
Marginal people, 57
Mass behavior, 30
Mass culture, 35
Mass media, 40
    communication, 24, 35–36
Mass society, 24–25, 33–34
Material culture, 19, 67–68, 79
    assessment for, 68–77
McDonaldization
    process, 20–21
    of society, 20
Media, 33
Mediascapes, 15–16
Mediated communication,
    40–41
Middle Class, 67–68
Mini-economic systems, 9
Minimal Phase Model of
    Globalization, 2–3
MNCs, 12
Models of communication,
    31–33
Modern culture, 18
Modern mass media, 42–43
    communication, 77
Modernity, 22, 25–26, 54, 67–68
    as process of cultural
      globalization, 22–23
Modernization, 50–51
"Modernization of Indian
    Tradition", 49
Multiculturalism, 3, 36
Multimedia, 41

National Education Policy 2020,
    India, 62
National Youth Policy (2021),
    67–68
Negative hyperglobalizers, 6
Neoliberal Economy, 67–68
Network intimacy, 37

Network Societies, 4
New communication research, trends of, 35–36
New Economic Policy, 67–68
New Media, 79
Nonmaterial culture, 67–68
  case of, 80–82

OBC respondents, 75
Online anonymity, 39
Overall Modernity Scale (O.M. Scale), 67–68, 80

Pluralism, 21
Political globalization, 12–13
Political organization, 10
Political process, 12–13
Popular culture, 35
Post-modernism, 1, 4
Postmodernity, 23
Postmodernization concept, 22–23
Primitive societies, 30–31
Print media, 26, 37, 41
Print/traditional media, 41–42
Process-agency approach, globalization as, 9–10
Protest movements, 13–14
Psychic mobility, 26–27

Radical feminism, 58
Read Only Web, 44
Reflexive modernity, 23
Regionalization, 50
Relative deterritorialization, 2
Respondents, socioeconomic background of, 68–77
"Rise of Network Societies", The, 4
Rural background respondents, 72–73
Rural–urban continuum, 17, 19

SC respondents, 75
Schools of globalization, 5–8
  hyperglobalizers, 5–6
  skeptics, 6–7
  transformationalists, 7–8

Schramm's model of development communication, 31–32
Second methodological concept, 7
Shannon Weaver's Model of Communication, 30–31
Skeptics, 5–7
SMCR model of communication, 30, 32–33
Social media(*see also* Mass media), 26, 41, 44–45
  and emerging adults, 36–37
  or new communication technologies, 44–46
Social mobilization, 26
Social networking sites, 45, 79
Social processes, 45–46
Social/Marxist feminism, 58
Society, 15, 24
Sociocultural transformation, 68
Sociopolitical system, 7–8
ST respondents, 74
Standardization of society, 34
Structural process, 10
  globalization as, 10–13
Supra territorial relations, 2
System-structure approach, globalization as, 9

Tangibility of culture, 19
Technoscape, 15–16
Territory-scale approach, globalization as, 9
The Second Gender, 57–58, 60–63
Time-space compression, 8
Time–space approach, globalization as, 8–9
Totalitarianism concept, 34–35
Traditional culture, 18
Traditional media, 30–31, 41–42
Traditional societies, 30–31
Traditionalism, 21
Transformationalists, 5, 7–8

Index

Transforming processes of culture, globalization in, 20–22
Transitional societies, 29
Transnational Corporations (TNC), 11
Tribes/tribal societies, 18
  in globalized cultural perspectives, 51–54

Ubuntu, 52–53
Unfair Global trade, 12
United Nations Economic Commission for Latin America and the Caribbean (UN ECLAC), 51
Universal knowledge systems, 3–4
Urbanization, 17, 34–35
  folk culture to, 17–19

Vernacular print media, 77–78
Virtual community, 37

Virtual culture, 25

WEB 1.0, 44
WEB 2.0 technologies, 45
WEB 3.0, 45
Western Capitalism, 11
Western civilizational ideologies, 52
Western imperialism, 6
Westernization, 7–8, 14
WhatsApp, 79
Women, 57, 63–64
  in contemporary India, 61–62
  empowerment, 61
  and modern cultures, 57–59
"World culture" systems, 3
World Trade Organization (WTO), 11
World Wide Web, 44

Yoga, 49–50
Youths, 66–68

Printed and bound by CPI Group (UK) Ltd, Croydon, CR0 4YY

30/10/2024

14583753-0003